# Strengthening Domestic Resource Mobilization

DIRECTIONS IN DEVELOPMENT
Public Sector Governance

# Strengthening Domestic Resource Mobilization

*Moving from Theory to Practice in Low- and Middle-Income Countries*

Raul Felix Junquera-Varela, Marijn Verhoeven, Gangadhar P. Shukla, Bernard Haven, Rajul Awasthi, and Blanca Moreno-Dodson

**WORLD BANK GROUP**

# Contents

## Boxes

## Figures

## Tables

# Preface

Domestic resource mobilization (DRM) is a core priority of the sustainable development agenda. The 2015 Addis Ababa Action Agenda on Financing for Development emphasized that the "mobilization and effective use of domestic resources … are central to our common pursuit of sustainable development." The Addis Tax Initiative, a multistakeholder partnership of more than 45 countries and organizations launched at the same conference, pledged "to double … support for technical cooperation in the area of taxation/domestic revenue mobilization by 2020." Under the United Nation's 2030 Agenda for Sustainable Development Goals, the international community committed to "… strengthen domestic resource mobilization, including through international support to developing countries, to improve domestic capacity for tax and other revenue collection."

DRM is also a priority for the World Bank and other international financial institutions. At the 2015 Addis Ababa conference, the World Bank and the International Monetary Fund (IMF) resolved to "strengthen … diagnostic tools, developing new methodologies where needed, to enable member countries to identify priority tax reforms and design the requisite support for their implementation." The World Bank has incorporated tax reforms into its technical assistance instruments and has more than 100 staff members supporting tax operations. Through the Platform for Collaboration on Tax, the World Bank also has coordinated its work with the IMF, the Organisation for Economic Co-operation and Development, and the United Nations to ensure common benchmarks for analysis, prevent duplication, share information, and design joint outputs.

As this report demonstrates, domestic resources are central to achieving development objectives. Many lower-income countries have the potential to increase their revenue collection by 2–4 percent of gross domestic product (GDP), without sacrificing equity or growth. This amount is not insignificant—the 2015 GDP of low-income and lower-middle-income countries was $6.3 trillion, which would translate into a revenue gain of US$125 billion to US$250 billion. In comparison, official development assistance totaled US$135 billion in 2015.

For some countries, increasing DRM could help them pass the 15 percent tax-to-GDP ratio, which is viewed as the minimum required to fund basic state functions, such as health care, education, public safety, and transportation. Indeed, 36 percent of International Development Association (IDA) countries and 70 percent of fragile and conflict-affected countries fall below this 15-percent baseline.

In addition to generating greater resources for public investment and spending, reform of tax policy and administration can also enhance overall governance. Expanding a country's DRM is likely to be politically feasible and sustainable only if it is associated with improved rule-of-law, accountability, and transparency standards. Cooperation with increased tax collection efforts requires public confidence in public expenditure. Moreover, increased tax collection capacity can improve the fairness of the tax system in eliminating exceptions or special treatment for those who were able to exploit the inadequacies of the previous system.

Looking toward the future, increased DRM efforts will face several challenges, from the structural features of the economy and the institutional distribution of power to more specific tax policy and administrative issues. Tax reform will need to be measured, not only on the basis of the overall quantity of tax collection, but also on the quality of tax composition. It will also require sustained political will from governments and broad support from the private sector and the wider public.

To support DRM as part of the sustainable development agenda, this report outlines how the World Bank can play a lead role in international assistance on reform of tax policy and administration in three areas:

- Enhancing the quality of tax systems (increasing tax collection but also minimizing economic distortions and reducing inequality)
- Strengthening the operational capacity of tax administrations in terms of both administrative and policy aspects
- Fostering social acceptance and legitimacy of the tax system, while improving public accountability, for example, by reaching out to civil society.

I hope that this report will be useful as a reference for all stakeholders contributing to this important agenda in the months and years ahead.

James A. Brumby
*Director, Governance Global Practice*
*World Bank*

# Acknowledgments

This book is a product of the Global Tax Team in the Equitable Growth, Finance, and Institutions Vice Presidency. It draws on a range of the World Bank's operational engagements in the areas of tax policy and administration.

The authors are grateful to Omowunmi Ladipo, Tuan Minh Le, Enrique Rojas, and Stephane Schlotterbeck for insightful comments and guidance as peer reviewers. Richard Stern also provided guidance and shared his extensive knowledge throughout the drafting process.

The authors thank Steven Webb for the annex on lessons learned in Bank operations. Bryan Christopher Land contributed his expertise on extractive industries, and Patricio V. Marquez provided key inputs on tobacco taxation. Francisco Lazzaro provided timely operational support and advice. Matthew Edward Collin contributed useful tax data and visualizations. Mary Fisk and Bart Szewczyk made significant editorial contributions.

The authors also thank Daniel J. Boyce, Guenter Heidenhof, and James A. Brumby for overall management and direction.

# About the Authors

**Raul Felix Junquera-Varela** is Global Lead on Domestic Revenue Mobilization and Lead Public Sector Specialist in the Governance Global Practice of the World Bank. He has more than 30 years of experience in public sector reform, with a particular focus on tax administration and customs. He held senior positions at the Spanish Revenue Agency from 1984 to 1998, including Director of a Regional Tax and Customs Office and Senior National Tax Auditor in the Large Taxpayer Office. He headed the Spanish Diplomatic Mission at the Inter-American Centre of Tax Administration and served as the Financial Advisor to the Spanish Embassy in Panama. In 2005, he joined the International Monetary Fund as Technical Assistance Advisor in the Revenue Administration Division of the Fiscal Affairs Department. His research interests include institution building and operational reform of revenue administrations, and he has authored numerous publications on these topics. He is an economist, a lawyer, and a certified public accountant.

**Marijn Verhoeven** is a Lead Economist and Cluster Lead with the World Bank Group's Governance Global Practice, where he leads work on domestic revenue mobilization and fiscal risk of state-owned enterprises and contributes to work streams on extractive industry governance, evidence-based public financial management reforms, political economy analysis, and public expenditure reviews. Before joining the World Bank, Verhoeven worked at the IMF, where he was the resident representative in Bangladesh and Deputy Division Chief of the Expenditure Policy Division. He was educated at Tilburg University in the Netherlands.

**Gangadhar P. Shukla** is Professor of the Practice of Public Policy at the Duke Center for International Development and Director of the Program on Tax Analysis and Revenue Forecasting. Previously, he was a lecturer and a Development Fellow at the Kennedy School of Government, Harvard University, and an Associate at the Harvard Institute for International Development. While at Harvard University, he taught courses at the Kennedy School and in the Economics Department, directed the Program on Tax Analysis and Revenue Forecasting, and provided technical assistance to more than a dozen countries in

Africa, Asia, and Latin America on tax policy and project evaluation. He previously served the government of India for 20 years in a variety of local, state, and central government executive positions—with considerable practical experience in local government finance, urban development, public sector management, financial management, budgeting, and revenue and expenditure analysis. He holds a PhD in political economics and government from Harvard University.

**Bernard Haven** is a Young Professional in the World Bank's Governance Global Practice, in the South Asia Region. Before coming to the World Bank, he was a diplomat with Global Affairs Canada. In Haiti, he was an economic adviser at the Canadian Embassy and led work on a tax and customs technical assistance program. In South Sudan, he headed the technical secretariat of a multidonor public administration trust fund. In Afghanistan, he was based at the Kandahar Provincial Reconstruction Team and the Canadian Embassy, supporting local governance and basic service delivery. He began his public service career at a tax services office of the Canada Revenue Agency in Quebec. He was educated at Calvin College, the London School of Economics, and the School of Oriental and African Studies at the University of London.

**Rajul Awasthi** is a Senior Public Sector Specialist, leading the tax policy and revenue administration work stream in the Europe and Central Asia region of the World Bank. He is also a member of the Global Tax Team of the World Bank Group. At the World Bank, he has worked on tax reform projects in almost 90 countries in East Africa, South Asia, Latin America and the Caribbean, Central and East Asia, and Europe. He worked as an adviser with the Finance Minister of India from 2004 to 2008, a period characterized by unprecedented economic growth and major reforms. He assisted the Finance Minister in macroeconomic management and in initiating tax administration and tax policy reforms, and he worked with the Investment Commission on developing India's foreign direct investment policy. He was an officer of the Indian Revenue Service for 10 years, where he held leadership roles in tax administration. He holds a master's degree in economics and public policy from Princeton University's Woodrow Wilson School of Public and International Affairs, and an MBA from the Indian Institute of Management, Ahmedabad, India.

**Blanca Moreno-Dodson** is a development macroeconomist with more than 25 years of World Bank experience, including worldwide operational and analytical work and regional expertise in Africa and Latin America. She specializes in providing macroeconomic and fiscal policy advice in developing countries, with a focus on growth, inequality, and poverty reduction. She has deep expertise in public expenditure analysis, fiscal sustainability, public finance, tax policy reforms, and transfer pricing. Previously, she worked as a junior economist at the European Union (European Commission and European Parliament). She has published extensively on these topics at the World Bank and in academic journals.

She has been a guest lecturer at the Universities of Duke and John Hopkins (United States), Aix-Marseille II (Université de la Méditerranée) and Clermont-Ferrand (France), and Navarra and Madrid (Spain) and is a frequent speaker at international development conferences and workshops. She holds a PhD and master of international economics and finance from the Aix-Marseille II, and a master of economics degree from the Autónoma University of Madrid.

# Abbreviations

| | |
|---|---|
| AAA | analytical and advisory activities |
| AEOI | automatic exchange of information |
| BEPS | base erosion and profit shifting |
| CIT | corporate income tax |
| CPIA | Country Policy and Institutional Assessment |
| DPL | development policy loan |
| DRM | domestic resource mobilization |
| EITI | Extractive Industries Transparency Initiative |
| EPZ | export processing zone |
| EU | European Union |
| G-20 | Group of Twenty |
| GDP | gross domestic product |
| HICs | high-income countries |
| HRM | human resource management |
| IAMTAX | Integrated Assessment Model for Tax Administration |
| ICT | information and communication technology |
| IDA | International Development Association |
| IFC | International Finance Corporation |
| IL | investment lending |
| IMF | International Monetary Fund |
| IT | information technology |
| LICs | low-income countries |
| LMICs | low- and middle-income countries |
| LTU | large taxpayer unit |
| MDG | Millennium Development Goal |
| MSMEs | micro, small, and medium enterprises |
| NRA | National Revenue Agency (Bulgaria) |
| NTLA | nonlending technical assistance |
| ODA | official development assistance |

| OECD | Organisation for Economic Co-operation and Development |
| PAYE | pay as you earn |
| PIT | personal income tax |
| POA | performance outcome area |
| PREM | Poverty Reduction and Economic Management |
| SAT | Servicio de Administración Tributaria (Tax Administration Service, Mexico) |
| SDG | Sustainable Development Goal |
| TADAT | Tax Administration Diagnostic Assessment Tool |
| TAMP | Transitional Assistance Management Program |
| TARP | tax administration reform project |
| TPU | tax policy unit |
| TTL | task team leader |
| UMICs | upper-middle-income countries |
| UN | United Nations |
| VAT | value added tax |

CHAPTER 1

# Introduction

This report presents an overview of current trends in tax policy, tax administration, and international taxation and provides a broad landscape of practical examples drawn from World Bank operations across Global Practices over the past several decades.[1] As a starting point for a more comprehensive research agenda, it is intended to play two roles: to provide guidance to World Bank staff working on related tax issues and to trigger a wider external dialogue through a forthcoming flagship report addressing strategic aspects of taxation in greater depth (World Bank 2017).

Public spending has consistently played a key role in the economic growth and development of most low- and middle-income countries (LMICs) and continues to do so today. This report analyzes the status of government revenues and identifies policy and administrative steps that may help to mobilize domestic resources in LMICs with a view to helping to frame the strategic position of the World Bank at this particular time. The suggestions are meant to support the role of the Bank in the context of the Addis Tax Initiative and the Sustainable Development Goals 2030 as well as to facilitate the collection of tax and non-tax revenue in order to provide LMICs with a stable and predictable fiscal environment.

## Domestic Resource Mobilization as an Instrument of Sustained and Inclusive Development

Domestic revenues can lead to improved development only if they are translated into productive and beneficial public expenditure. For this reason, both sides of the fiscal equation—revenue and expenditure—need to be examined together. However, both governments and donors tend to analyze revenue generation and public spending separately, except when it comes to their joint effects on macroeconomic stability and income inequality. As a result, either revenues are taken as given or spending is considered without addressing the tax policy and administrative measures needed to yield the requisite resources.

Considering tax and expenditure policy issues jointly greatly enhances the likelihood of achieving revenue sufficiency for sustained economic and social development. The two goals are linked and should be addressed in tandem. Both revenue and expenditure reforms should therefore be embedded in broader public financial management reforms. When this is done, domestic resource mobilization (DRM) rightly becomes a development tool for generating revenues to support sustained and inclusive economic development.

At subnational levels in most LMICs, public expenditures have been growing in quantum and importance. The provincial and municipal governments provide critical services to the population and need commensurate resources to be able to do that. They may use some of the same revenue instruments as are used by the central government, such as income tax, value added tax, or sales tax, but they also use a different set of taxes, such as property taxes, and nontax instruments, such as user fees, that constitute an important source of revenue. Sometimes, they receive part of the rents from natural resources. The role of subnational governments in mobilizing revenue as well as in spending on service provision should therefore be part of the broad DRM agenda.

## Taxation as a Plank of State Building

The state-building process involves ongoing negotiations between the state and its citizens. On the one hand, tax reform is influenced and guided by the political economy; on the other hand, taxation can be instrumental in the state-building process in a variety of ways, particularly in LMICs. As government depends on taxes and on the prosperity of the people, it has a strong incentive to promote economic growth and engage with the public. This dependence leads to accountability and responsiveness on the part of the state.[2]

Taxation may also help to introduce good practices within different parts of government. For example, in many countries, the introduction of unique taxpayer identification numbers has strengthened other parts of the public and private sectors, including municipal governments and commercial banks. Tax systems build databases that are essential for broader economic and administrative management. Tax reforms emphasize merit-based hiring and performance management, which are highly relevant to other agencies and departments in government. Tax reform should, therefore, be seen as an essential part of state building.

## Organization of the Report

Chapter 2 provides an overview of the opportunities and challenges presented by DRM, covering its centrality to the sustainable development agenda, revenue trends and gaps, and requirements for tax reform. Chapters 3 and 4 detail outstanding issues in reforming tax policy and in modernizing and reforming tax administration. Chapter 5 concludes by outlining a strategy for the World Bank to engage and lead on DRM.

## Notes

1. It does not cover the revenue functions of customs, which are addressed in other World Bank research.
2. For a discussion of the core elements of a governance-focused tax reform agenda, see Prichard (2010).

## References

Prichard, Wilson. 2010. "Taxation and State Building: Towards a Governance Focused Tax Reform Agenda." IDS Working Paper 341, Institute of Development Studies, Brighton, U.K.

World Bank. 2017. "Board Update: Domestic Resource Mobilization (DRM) and Illicit Financial Flows (IFFs)." World Bank, Washington, DC, February.

**CHAPTER 2**

# Domestic Resource Mobilization: Opportunities and Challenges

## DRM as a Key to Economic Growth and Development

Domestic resource mobilization (DRM) has become a core priority of the sustainable development agenda. The 2015 Addis Ababa Action Agenda on Financing for Development emphasized the importance of DRM, noting that the "mobilization and effective use of domestic resources … are central to our common pursuit of sustainable development." On the revenue side, the only reliable and sustained sources of government revenue are taxes and some non-tax revenue instruments, such as royalties and resource rents from extractive industries and, to a limited extent, user fees for public services, generally delivered by local governments. Public sector investments through state-owned enterprises have not been a reliable source of revenue in low- and middle-income countries (LMICs); instead, they have often been a drag on the budget. On the expenditure side, legal obligations often make it difficult to lower administrative overhead, curtail debt servicing, and reduce transfer payments. Thus, lack of sufficient domestic revenue mobilization often results in the cutback of new capital assets and the poor maintenance and operation of existing assets. These cutbacks have an adverse impact on both the level and the quality of present-day services as well as the rate of future economic growth and development.

In most LMICs, particularly low-income countries (LICs), government revenues fall short of the rising need for public expenditures and have to be supplemented through borrowing, multilateral development assistance, or both. Excessive public borrowing from domestic sources can crowd out borrowing and investments by the private sector, with adverse effects on economic growth. Foreign borrowing inherently raises the interest rate on future debt and often leads to high indebtedness. In order to service the loans and avoid falling into a debt trap, the funds borrowed from abroad must be invested in projects and programs that are productive and economically viable. Such investments require capacity for project appraisal and expenditure analysis on the part of line ministries and the ministry of economy and planning, which is weak in many LMICs.

Official development assistance (ODA) is clearly finite and fluctuates over time, creating uncertainty for recipient countries about planning, budgeting, and expenditures in the public sector. Thus, a chronic and substantial dependence on debt and foreign aid raises serious concerns about the sustainability of government spending and its implications for future economic growth. ODA has uncertain impacts on long-term DRM. Grants may fully displace domestic revenues, but a better understanding of the links between foreign assistance and domestic revenues is needed so that aid supports countries' own efforts to generate tax revenue. Continued, long-term dependence on aid is unlikely to be conducive to enhanced DRM (IMF 2011).[1]

### The Challenge of Funding the Sustainable Development Goals

The Sustainable Development Goals (SDGs)—the post-2015 development agenda espoused in the 2015 United Nations (UN) Summit, which replaced the Millennium Development Goals (MDGs) of 2000—have raised the bar for all nations, particularly LICs. They aim to meet the dual challenges of eradicating global poverty, on the one hand, and protecting the environment, on the other. Picking up the unfinished agenda of the MDGs, the SDGs have set ambitious goals that combine economic growth and social development with environmental sustainability. The financial resources required to achieve the SDGs, therefore, far exceed the resources presently devoted to development expenditures. While the goal of transforming the world by 2030 is both attractive and desirable, funding these goals clearly poses unprecedented challenges, particularly for LMICs.

According to the Intergovernmental Committee of Experts on Sustainable Development Financing, providing a social safety net to eradicate extreme poverty globally would cost roughly US$66 billion a year, while improving infrastructure to protect the environment could cost as much as US$7 trillion a year (UN General Assembly 2014). LMICs, particularly low-income countries, rely on public international finance to fund their development agendas. However, in 2013 only five donors from the Organisation for Economic Co-operation and Development (OECD) Development Assistance Committee met the UN's longstanding target of spending 0.7 percent of gross national income on ODA, and ODA reached only US$135 billion in net terms at its peak amount. Meanwhile, LICs have followed a consistent pattern in which they lose access to concessional loans, but do not expand domestic taxes and foreign private and market-related public borrowing enough to compensate for the loss of ODA.

Even if the annual ODA level were to double, LMICs would still face a large financing gap with regard to the cost of implementing the SDGs. According to the Intergovernmental Committee of Experts, resources generated from the private sector, through tax reforms and a crackdown on illicit financial flows and corruption, are vital to achieving these goals. Most development spending occurs at the national level in the form of public resources, received largely from private businesses, finance, and investment. The SDG agenda has shifted the focus of sustainable development from relying solely on "billions" in ODA to unlocking "trillions" in internal and external, private and public capital (Development Committee 2015). This shift in financing for development ultimately requires strengthening the sources of domestic revenue.

### Inevitability of Domestic Resource Mobilization

During the UN Addis Ababa Financing for Development conference in July 2015, all of the participating nations seemed to acknowledge the complexity of obtaining development finance from households, businesses, and governments. Thus, DRM reemerged as a key source of funding for national development plans for LMICs. At its core, the topic of DRM through taxation is once again on the global front burner (McArthur 2015).[2]

The experience of LMICs also shows that there are ways to improve DRM, including through more efficient taxation and improved management of extractives revenues. Since 1990, while average government revenue in high-income countries (HICs) has more or less plateaued, in LICs it has increased from 18 percent to 21 percent of gross domestic product (GDP), with similar increases posted by lower-middle-income countries and by upper-middle-income countries (UMICs).

However, domestic revenues still fall short of what is needed to support a more robust development agenda in countries where poverty is highest and needs are most pronounced. Countries with some of the lowest revenue-to-GDP ratios are also those where the vast majority of the world's extremely poor live—Bangladesh, China, India, and Nigeria all have tax-to-GDP ratios below 15 percent. Over the past two decades, however, trends in revenues and taxes have gradually improved in countries across all income categories, as discussed in the next section.

## Trends in Total Revenues and Taxes

Revenue trends are typically reported using the tax-to-GDP ratio over time. However, this measure has pitfalls mainly because revenue collection figures sometimes vary by source and the computation of GDP figures itself is often questionable. Some countries (for example, Ghana) go through a process of reestimating GDP figures that affects this ratio considerably. This metric also assumes away differences in countries' socioeconomic structure, institutional arrangements, and demographic trends. Ideally, tax effort is a better indicator.[3] In practice, most available revenue collection data use the tax-to-GDP ratio, so the calculations presented here also use this ratio.

This section presents trends in government revenues as well as tax revenues (1990–2013) for both HICs and LMICs. (For further details on the type of tax revenue by country income group and region during 1990–2012, see appendix A.)

Total revenue increased from 18 percent to 21 percent of GDP in LICs during the period between 1990 and 2014. Trends were similar in both lower-middle-income countries and UMICs, while revenue growth was generally static in HICs.

In LICs, total tax revenue increased from 11 percent to 14 percent of GDP during the period between 1990 and 2014 (figure 2.2). The gradual increase in total tax revenue, primarily owing to an increase in income taxes and value added tax (VAT), contributed to much of the growth in total revenue in LICs.

While LICs and lower-middle-income countries increased the amount of revenue received from VAT and income taxes, UMICs and HICs shifted away from income taxes and toward consumption taxes. The aggregate growth in income tax—individual and .corporate—was small, increasing only slightly from 11 percent to 12 percent in HICs and from 6 percent to 7 percent in UMICs between 1990 and 2013. In the same period, the goods and services tax rose from 8 percent to 12 percent in HICs and from 5 percent to 15 percent in UMICs, with a similar increase in the VAT.

VAT collections have increased in countries at all income levels since the beginning of the new millennium. LICs introduced VAT around the turn of the century, and VAT revenue has grown steadily since then. Since VAT revenue also rose in lower-middle-income countries and in UMICs, the average VAT was around 7 percent of GDP for countries at all income levels in 2013, up from 3 percent of GDP in 1990. The increase in VAT and excise taxes generally has affected consumption; as a result, the tax burden is being borne by the middle- and working-class population. The combination of higher taxes on consumption

**Figure 2.1  Total Revenue as a Percentage of GDP, by Country Income Group, 1990–2014**

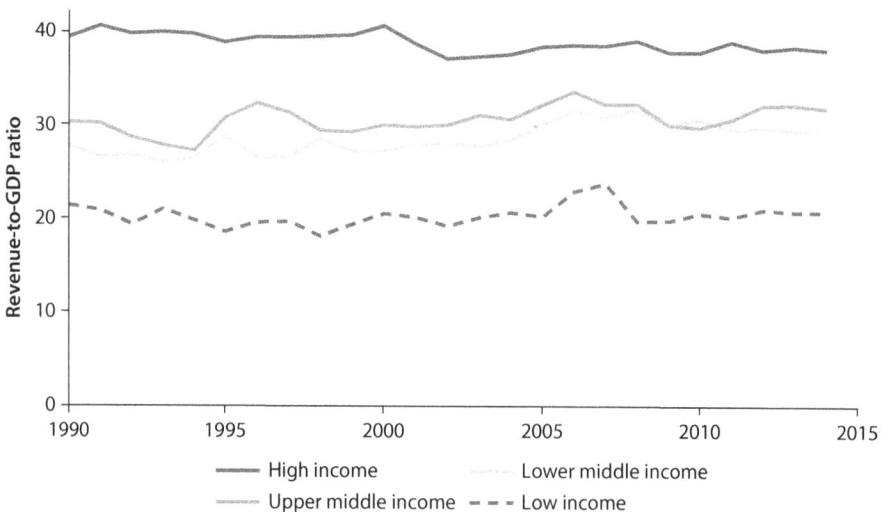

*Source:* International Monetary Fund, World Revenue Longitudinal Dataset, http://data.imf.org/.
*Note:* GDP = gross domestic product.

**Figure 2.2 Tax Revenue (Excluding Social Contributions) as a Percentage of GDP, by Country Income Group, 1990–2014**

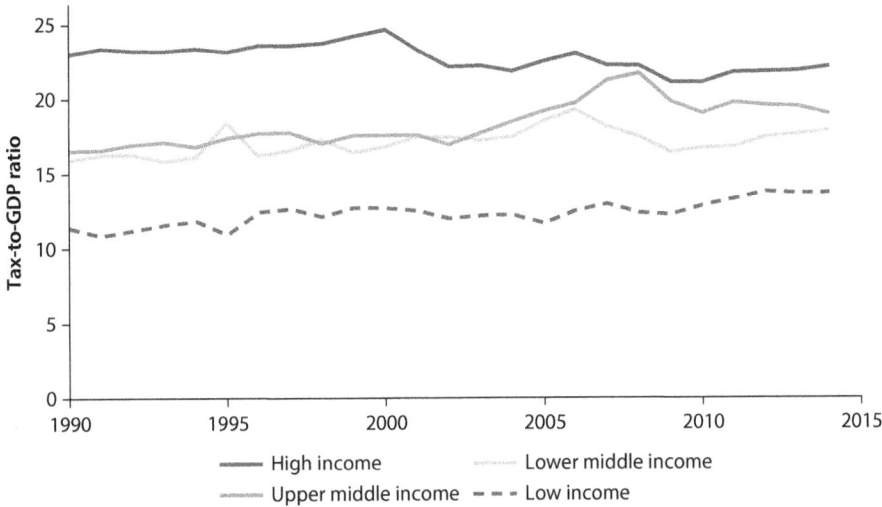

*Source:* International Monetary Fund, World Revenue Longitudinal Dataset, http://data.imf.org/.
*Note:* GDP = gross domestic product.

and lower taxes on income has eroded the overall progressivity of taxes. During this period, UMICs and HICs witnessed a steady decline in trade transaction taxes, largely due to trade liberalization. In addition, countries compensated for lower trade taxes with higher VAT.

Countries can close the revenue gap in several ways, as discussed in the following section.

## Closing the Revenue Gap

Revenue gaps persist in a country for four main reasons: low tax capacity, lack of a "good" tax system, low tax effort, and globalization.

### Low Tax Capacity of the Economy

One reason a country does not collect sufficient tax revenues is due to the low tax capacity of its economy. Even if everyone agrees that DRM is a key to sustainable development and that tax revenues as a percentage of GDP should be higher, can LMICs tax more? While the size of government (and taxation) is a political choice, the prevailing level of economic growth and structural characteristics of the economy affect the feasibility and costs of collecting taxes. Cost-effective tax administration is affected by the availability or absence of "tax handles," such as level of per capita income, literacy rate, urbanization, presence of a large corporate sector, existence of a tourism industry, presence of natural resources, and size of the formal sector.[4]

Tax capacity is hard to change in the short run. Nevertheless, it is important to estimate tax capacity before assessing whether the existing tax capacity and revenue potential are being exploited fully and effectively. Starting in the early 1970s, the International Monetary Fund ran a series of regressions using cross-country data from LMICs to arrive at equations for estimating a country's tax capacity based on its parameters, such as per capita income and size of the various economic sectors as a share of GDP. These regressions were followed by several other empirical studies considering the question of tax capacity in LMICs (Le, Moreno-Dodson, and Bayraktar 2009). Most of these studies concluded that, in economic terms, most countries have underutilized tax capacity and can indeed tax more in order to reach their full revenue potential. The main issue is whether there is political will to exploit that tax capacity on a sustained basis (Tanzi 1987).

To estimate the tax capacity of any country, it is often difficult to collect large-scale data from a group of countries and to run a regression. As an alternative, it may be easier and more practical to compile data on revenue collection as a percentage of GDP for a select group of countries with similar economic characteristics for each kind of tax—VAT, personal income tax (PIT), corporate income tax (CIT), and excises—and then to compare the sum total, taken as an estimate of tax capacity of the country in question.

### Lack of a "Good" Tax System

Another reason for a country's revenue gap is the lack of a "good" tax system, which features four basic elements: equity, economic efficiency, technical efficiency, and revenue stability.

First, an equitable tax system should have both horizontal and vertical equity—people in equal circumstances should be taxed equally, while those with greater ability to pay should pay a higher percentage of their income in taxes. A tax system that taxpayers perceive to be fair commands better compliance and raises more revenue. Also, improving equity in the enforcement of taxation is particularly effective not only for neutralizing public opposition but also for creating some degree of support for tax reform.

Second, economic efficiency entails minimizing tax-induced distortions in consumption, savings, work effort, and investment. With regard to economic efficiency, the high costs of taxation are related mostly to high tax rates and large differentials in tax rates across sectors. So, a tax system with fewer and more moderate tax rates imposes lower deadweight loss or excess burden.

Third, technical efficiency demands low costs of both administration and taxpayer compliance. Low costs may, in turn, be achieved by simplifying the tax structure, enhancing awareness and transparency, and streamlining administrative procedures. Many tax reforms have sought to raise more tax revenue without paying adequate attention to improving the tax system and facilitating compliance. The costs of compliance for businesses are often nontrivial and may constitute a significant share of taxes owed.[5] In the World Bank's investment climate assessment survey, almost 40 percent of businesses overall said that they consider the tax administration to be a major constraint. This is especially true in LMICs (World Bank 2009).

Finally, stability of the tax system basically means that the rate of revenue growth should keep pace with the rate of economic growth in the country. This stability can be achieved more easily if the tax base is well diversified and broad and encompasses the sectors that are contributing to economic growth.

The lack of a "good" tax system indicates a poor tax policy, which, of course, is possible to remedy through a well-designed and properly implemented tax policy reform. This reform would, in turn, require the existence of a tax policy unit or creation of a change management unit within the ministry of finance with the necessary entrepreneurial and technical skills. Given the proper level of political support, a sound tax policy reform can be accomplished over a span of three to five years.

### Low Tax Effort

The third reason for a revenue gap is a low tax effort, which is defined as the ratio of actual tax collection to tax capacity. An alternative but effective approach—estimating the tax base (for each kind of tax), forecasting different kinds of tax revenues, and comparing them with actual intake—could be used to assess the tax effort in most LMICs. This approach has the advantage of yielding an approximate idea of tax revenue performance. In any case, a low tax effort basically points to a weak tax administration and low level of compliance on the part of domestic taxpayers. Compliance could be poor for a variety of reasons, including a culture of tax avoidance and tax evasion and a perception of poor or zero linkage between taxes paid and public services provided.

To improve tax administration, a government usually adopts a two-prong approach. First, the institutions of tax administration and compliance mechanisms need to be strengthened; this effort would include enhancing the procedural and legal framework covering assessment, collection, audit, sanctions, appeals, record keeping, use of information technology, and reward and punishment structure of the civil service; the disclosure requirement of firms; and the accounting conventions used by them. Sometimes corruption and rent seeking hamper the performance of tax administration. Reorganizing and segmenting the tax administration to handle large, medium, and small taxpayers separately and improving the use of information technology may help to improve tax performance. Improving data management and analysis may help to lower the costs of compliance and to reduce the scope for corruption and collusion.

Second, a capacity-building program for personnel of the tax administration at different levels and a sustained campaign of taxpayer service and taxpayer education and awareness may be necessary. Reducing compliance costs and adopting a customer-oriented focus are the key to better compliance and collection.

Reforming and strengthening both tax administration and compliance are again a doable, though time-consuming, process, just like tax policy reform.

### *Globalization and International Trade and Capital Flows*

The final reason for a revenue gap is globalization and the accompanying growth in international trade and capital flows, which have increased the difficulty of taxing transnational transactions. Businesses now have great scope for aggressive tax planning through tax shelters, profit shifting, and abusive transfer pricing practices. For instance, U.S. Senate investigations in 2013 exposed cases of many highly profitable multinationals that did not pay tax in any country and were doing so in a perfectly legal way. Similarly, the European Union has recently started legal action against several multinational enterprises operating in its territory but shifting profits elsewhere.

For instance, a highly profitable unit of Apple was registered in Ireland, controlled from the United States, and not paying tax in any country. This "stateless-income" structure was quite legal, highlighting the prevalence of big loopholes in the global system for taxing multinationals. Countries such as Ireland and the Netherlands allow big companies to register local subsidiaries even though they have no physical presence in the country. The Netherlands alone has more than 10,000 "letterbox" firms in Amsterdam alone. Naturally there has been growing public outrage over firms not paying their "fair share."

The reason behind such gaps and loopholes is clear: the set of national laws, rules, and bilateral treaties governing how much tax a multinational company owes and to whom are outdated and inadequate. These rules and laws were designed for the manufacturing sectors, but businesses today have become highly digitalized and service-oriented companies, holding intangible assets and intellectual property. These businesses are easier to move from subsidiaries in high-tax jurisdictions to subsidiaries in low-tax regions. This ability has enabled some multinationals to engage in aggressive tax planning.

According to a conservative estimate of the OECD, the resulting revenue losses to governments globally is about US$240 billion annually, which amounts to about 10 percent of global CIT receipts. The share of profits that U.S. firms alone book in low-tax havens has almost doubled in the last three decades. This circumstance effectively reduces the actual tax rate these companies pay relative to the statutory rate in the United States. America's 500 largest firms hold more than US$2 trillion in profits offshore because, according to U.S. tax laws, the profits that companies make abroad are taxable in America only when they are repatriated (Zucman 2015).

In HICs, the problem arises mainly due to the difficulty of taxing intangibles and e-commerce. In LICs, there is the added difficulty of taxing extractive industries, which is significant in addition to other sector-related challenges, thereby yielding low fiscal revenues and allowing multinational companies to capture a high share of the rents.

Coupled with an asymmetry of capacity between businesses and tax administrations, the problem of taxing transnational firms gives rise to new challenges for tax administrations, particularly in LMICs, and adversely affects revenue collection.

## Summary
DRM therefore calls for long-term measures to bolster tax capacity and tax effort. Improved tax policy and administration are essential for achieving fiscal stability, economic growth, and poverty reduction in LMICs and can help to reduce long-term aid dependency. Unfortunately, there are no shortcuts for achieving these goals. In the short run, however, steps may be taken to strengthen tax policy and tax administration and to implement a revenue-forecasting system, as discussed in the next section.

## Challenges in Increasing Domestic Resource Mobilization in Low-Income Countries

LICs face two broad categories of challenges: (a) structural and institutional issues and (b) policy and administrative issues.

### Structural and Institutional Challenges
Several factors in a country, ranging from the nature of the economy to the political setup and the quality of governance, have an impact on revenue mobilization. These factors are especially challenging, as they are difficult to alter in the short run.

#### Structural Features of an Economy
Several structural features of an economy contribute to the ability of a country to generate fiscal revenues, including (a) per capita income; (b) share of domestic trade, imports, and exports; (c) degree of urbanization; (d) level of development of the corporate sector; (e) importance of the tourism industry; (f) share of agriculture in GDP and size of the informal sector; (g) existence of an extractive sector, including mining, oil, and gas; (h) levels of literacy, education, and human capital; (i) establishment of tax practitioners and accounting professionals; and (j) well-developed information technology, among others. All of these features help to shape revenue mobilization results. While a few of these factors, such as the existence or lack of extractive industries, may prove to be rigid, most of them diminish as the economy evolves. The government can obviously play a vital role in facilitating and fostering the necessary changes.

#### The Political Environment and Impact of Interest Groups
Political leadership plays a major role in revenue mobilization. Tax reform and technical assistance restricted to technical, apolitical aspects of taxation have failed to capture the reality of policy making and revenue collection in many countries. This failure is rooted in the fact that tax reform affects the distribution of resources and wealth and almost invariably confronts strong vested interests

that oppose the reforms. If there is a committed leadership, both within and outside the ministry of finance and the tax administration, tax reform is more likely to succeed.

As such, it is important for reforms to be informed by an understanding of political opportunities and constraints, as this understanding may guide the content, priority, timing, and strategy of reforms. The experience of many countries shows that, even after the formal tax structure and tax administration are reformed, levels of tax collection can remain unchanged unless there is sustained political will, local ownership, and adequate sequencing of implementation. Taxation, by its nature, has a political dimension, and all the rationality of a "good" tax policy and administration comes to naught if the reform is not properly presented to the people and supported by the political leaders.

Given the proper political environment and support, the government can extract revenues from the citizens and deliver public spending programs, including public investment to promote economic growth and development. The political dimension is therefore of paramount importance in any kind of tax and revenue reform.

Interest groups in every country exert subtle and sometimes blatant influence on tax policy, tax administration, and expenditure decisions made through the budgeting process. Most tax changes confront strong vested interests that stand to lose from the proposed changes. These vested interests usually comprise economic and political elites who are quite influential and capable of blocking reforms. Generally, it is difficult to mobilize public support for any kind of tax reform, which is often seen as threatening, even by those who are unaffected by or stand to gain from the proposed changes in the long run.

Sometimes the people or party in power use tax instruments to favor constituents and punish opponents. This favoritism is quite common in LMICs. Both interest groups and vested interests may lead the people in power to grant excessive exemptions and incentives "in the name of" equity and investment promotion. This behavior leads to substantial tax expenditures and loss of revenue.

### Corruption and Rent-Seeking Behavior in Administration and Politics

There are two levels of principal-agent relationship in taxation. At the first level, the people are the "principal," through their role in electing governments, and the tax department is the "agent" of the people and the government. At the second level, in the process of revenue collection, the role is reversed, and the tax department is the "principal," while taxpayers are the "agent." Just as in any principal-agent relationship, the agents may develop their own agenda, including inappropriate behavior, rent seeking, and corruption.

Corruption in government in general and in taxation in particular adversely affects the development and performance of the private sector. It raises transaction costs and uncertainty in doing business, and it can constitute a significant "tax" on the private sector. In LICs, motivation to earn illegal income may be strong because civil service salaries are low or declining. Sometimes the tax department along with other government agencies may even raise revenues for their political masters. This naturally adversely affects the mobilization of national revenue.

One way to address the problem of rent seeking and corruption in tax administration is to improve awareness among taxpayers and increase transparency in the application of rules and procedures. It is often very difficult for the general public to access even basic information on revenue collection. At the very least, people should be able to obtain data on total tax collections, disaggregated by type of tax and region.

## Tax Policy and Administrative Issues

Some common features of LMICs are responsible for poor revenue mobilization. The main tax policy elements are summarized here.

### Complexity of the Tax System

With gradual and incremental changes in tax laws in pursuit of higher tax revenues, as well as in response to political pressure, tax structures often become complex in nature. Sometimes governments favor minor taxes and fees, which are costly to comply with and administer, do not generate enough revenues, and end up becoming "nuisance taxes." Sometimes they favor major taxes that have a narrow base and high rates, which can be less effective in raising revenue, while increasing the costs of both administration and taxpayer compliance.

Some countries have a VAT base that is too narrow, has too many rates, and has a low threshold. Though intended to generate higher revenues or promote greater equity, such VATs neither mobilize more revenue nor promote equity.

The PIT is generally weak, has multiple exemptions, and is poorly managed. Apart from low per capita income and a large informal sector, including farmers and small businesses, lack of capacity for self-assessment and compliance is a significant hurdle. Consequently, the tax base is quite narrow, and scheduler taxes on specific sectors and taxation of high-income individuals become more important. This tax is seldom a good source of revenue in LMICs.

The CIT often has a narrow base focusing on foreign and large domestic companies and complicated depreciation and carry-forward provisions. To make matters worse, the CIT is generally replete with tax incentives, including tax holidays and free trade zones, that undermine the revenue potential without necessarily promoting investment.

Applying the CIT to multinationals is always difficult, as such firms have greater avenues for abusive transfer pricing and tax planning, leading to erosion of the revenue base and profit shifting. The problem is more pronounced in the presence of a weak legislative framework as well as an asymmetry of capacity and information between the tax administration and transnational companies.

In LMICs, interest groups pressure governments to grant exemptions under all taxes. Granting exemptions in a few cases results in gradual exemption creep, jeopardizing revenues and hindering sound tax administration without providing any social or economic benefits.

Informality is pervasive in LMICs, and taxation of micro, small, and medium enterprises (MSMEs), many of which operate informally, is a major challenge. For them, it may be necessary to establish a simplified tax regime and to link taxation to some benefits such as preference in institutional financing. However, a simplified tax regime gives rise to perverse incentives: MSMEs find it difficult to switch to the category of larger taxpayers, while large firms have an incentive to abuse the simplified regime.

In many resource-rich countries with large extractive industries, there is a lack of prudent selection of both fiscal instruments (such as income tax, resource rent tax, and import duties) and nontax instruments (such as royalties, bonuses, and government equity). While the statutory income tax rate is very high in a few countries (85 percent in Nigeria), effective rates in general are dismally low. In some cases, the rate of royalty is low or linked to profit or operating margins of the company, substantially reducing the rate of royalty. Equity participation by host governments seldom yields tax dividends, while increasing the risk to government. In addition, some countries suffer from a poor institutional setup and incentive structures that drive and fuel rent seeking and corruption. Such setups adversely affect revenue mobilization and create leaks in the value chain from the initial stage of licensing and extraction to the final stage of budgeting and expenditures. In such cases, the key challenge is to determine how to exit an adverse setup after decades of oil and mineral production.

In countries with a substantial extractive industries sector, international tax issues become particularly significant. Investors seek to obtain higher revenues up-front to satisfy lenders that the oil and mining operations will be able to meet repayments. Some of these investors aggressively resort to tax-saving instruments. Also, while multinationals can draw on the international expertise of tax accountants and lawyers, tax administrations often suffer from lack of effective tax laws and poor implementation, compromising on revenue collections.

Land and property are poorly exploited in LMICs. At the subnational or local levels of government, property taxes are often poorly designed, use faulty or outdated valuation systems, and are poorly implemented.

### Rigidities in Tax Administration

Tax administration may also suffer from rigidities affecting DRM, including the inability to forecast revenue accurately or at all; the setting of unrealistic revenue targets; the failure to assess the tax base, tax potential, or tax gap; and the passage of purely technical reforms of the tax administration. These are mentioned in turn.

Revenue forecasting is perhaps the weakest link in the chain between tax structure and revenue collected. Apart from estimating tax revenues for budgeting purposes, revenue forecasting is crucial for analyzing the impact of tax policies and economic changes or shocks. Presently, some LMICs have a superficial forecasting structure and do not follow a systematic approach.

In some cases, the forecasting exercise is done by a few individuals situated in the tax administration or the ministry of finance, who simply increase last year's forecast or actual tax collections by next year's expected GDP growth rate.

In some countries, next year's budget expenditures are estimated through call circulars to all the ministries, departments, and agencies. Expected borrowing and deficit financing are subtracted from total estimated budgetary expenditures, and the remaining amount is assigned to the tax department as next year's revenue targets. Line ministries often begin to spend on the basis of demands they have submitted to the ministry of finance even before the budget is passed. A revenue target without any basis or link to the state of the economy leads to unprofessional practices and destroys the integrity of the tax system. For these reasons, a sound revenue-forecasting system is essential. Sometimes, lack of good data is cited as the reason for no or poor forecasts. However, the link between data availability and revenue forecasting is two-way. Having revenue forecasting in place should lead to a good-quality database.

Apart from setting realistic collection targets, revenue forecasting is also an instrument for estimating the tax base and calculating the tax gap. With a good-quality revenue forecast, it is possible to measure the extent to which tax revenue potential has been realized, giving an "indication" of the tax effort. Revenue forecasts also are useful for establishing a benchmark for monitoring collection, stimulating effort, and measuring the performance of the revenue department, which can then be linked to an incentive scheme.

Some LMICs have focused on reforming and strengthening the traditional functions of tax administrations. That effort includes putting in place a sound system of tax assessment and an efficient mechanism of enforcement. Since self-assessment is now in force for most types of taxes in LMICs, emphasis is placed on creating an effective tax audit system and using risk-based audit techniques. Finally, a dispute resolution apparatus is established for filing appeals. What is generally missing is a taxpayer focus and a strategy for better compliance management.

## Reforming Tax Systems for Domestic Resource Mobilization

With renewed emphasis on DRM, the focus naturally turns to reform of both tax policy and tax administration. Until the 1970s, most reforms focused on tax structure, that is, on the tax base and tax rates. It was common for most countries to have high marginal income tax rates as well as high and variable coverage and rate structure of indirect taxes; this is typically not the case anymore. Tax reforms in the 1980s and 1990s began to focus on administrative issues as well. In more recent times, tax administration and taxpayer compliance have become an additional element of tax reforms. Comprehensive tax reform packages, however, have become more complex in nature, aiming to achieve multiple goals that not only seek to collect more revenue but also consider numerous policy administration trade-offs.

### Tax Reform to Achieve Objectives beyond Revenue Generation

Tax reform is an exercise in reconciling and arriving at a compromise among competing objectives, namely, equity, efficiency, macroeconomic stability, and environmental sustainability.[6] It is not simply a matter of collecting more revenue; rather, any reform should seek to enhance the quality of the tax system as a whole. In addition, it is essential to sustain revenue increases over the long run. Thus, strengthening tax administration and building capacity in the public sector are essential to achieving all of these objectives.

### Tax Reform to Enhance Government Responsiveness and Accountability

Taxation can provide an incentive for citizens and government to bargain and enter into a mutually beneficial "fiscal contract." In this contract, citizens accept and comply with taxes, while the government ensures the rule of law and provides public services. Citizens receive improved governance, while the state receives more predictable tax revenues. While this may be perceived as some sort of political concession by the government in the short term, it may turn out to be a mutually beneficial strategy in the long term (Moore 2008). Citizens are more willing to pay taxes if they observe real benefits in the form of local services.[7]

Several factors facilitate this process: (a) an equitable tax structure; (b) improved equity in enforcement and tax administration; (c) public awareness, transparency, and taxpayer services; (d) clearer link between taxation and public expenditure; and (e) constructive civil society engagement with tax issues. These issues should be at the core of policy and administrative reforms.

### Tax Structure Reform

Many past reforms have tried to achieve economic neutrality; in other words, to minimize the economic and social distortions caused by taxation, while maximizing revenue collection. Several measures have been adopted by many LMICs: an effort to broaden the tax base by reducing exemptions and exclusions; a shift away from trade taxes and toward goods and services taxes, including a combination of excises and VAT; a lowering of the CIT and PIT rates and a partial integration of the two taxes; and a general simplification of the tax code.

Several issues with respect to reforming tax structures today remain outstanding: low share of income taxes in total collection; prevalence of tax incentives and the resulting tax expenditures; challenges of dealing with informality and difficulty in taxing MSMEs; absence of a sound revenue-forecasting system and tax gap analysis; complexities of exploiting natural resources, particularly minerals, oil, and gas; and issues regarding the design of "sin" taxes (tobacco taxes, in particular) and environmental taxes (OECD 2010). Recently there has also been a move toward decentralization of revenue-raising functions, although this process is still in its early stages.

### Tax Administration Reform

Institutions of tax administration and compliance include a vast canvas of procedural and legal frameworks covering assessment, collection, audit, sanctions, appeals and dispute resolution, disclosure requirements of firms, record keeping, and accounting conventions. While more attention is being paid to these issues, emphasis is also being placed on reorganizing tax agencies from organization by type of tax to organization by core function and, more recently, by tax segments, specifically large, medium, and small taxpayers. Autonomy from the civil service and creation of revenue authorities have been major features in the last couple of decades in several countries of Africa and Latin America. It is expected that this autonomy will improve the performance of tax administrations by reducing political interference, increasing flexibility, and improving wages and working conditions.

Improving compliance management is recognized as being as important as strengthening the tools of administration. Improved data management and better analysis with the use of information technology has helped to lower compliance costs, enhance transparency, and reduce corruption and collusion. More attention is now being paid to taxpayer services, taxpayer awareness and education, customer orientation, and understanding of taxpayer behavior. While all of these are great initiatives, their implementation requires greater funding and a basic change in the mind-set of tax administrators. Finally, developing a diagnostic tool for assessing the health of the entire tax system and an overall human resource management strategy for the tax administration is of paramount importance.

The following chapters analyze tax policy and tax administration reform and outline a strategic role on DRM for the World Bank. Appendix B provides a technical note on benchmarks for a good tax system and for assessment of major tax regimes and tax administrations in LMICs.

## Notes

1. Government revenues may be reported with grants both included and excluded.
2. For a report on what happened at the conference and commitments made, see McArthur (2015).
3. Tax effort is the ratio of actual tax take divided by the tax capacity of the country. It estimates tax capacity using data from similar economies. Tax capacity depends on the basic structure and economic features of the country. Estimating tax effort is not straightforward, while computing tax-to-GDP ratios is simple.
4. Kaldor (1963) answered "yes" to this question in 1963, stating that even the poorest countries had enough economic and administrative capacity to tax more; whether or not a country does so depends on its political institutions. More recently, several tax economists have questioned the desirability of having a larger public sector.
5. Alm, Sanchez, and De Juan (1995) estimate that the compliance costs of certain taxes could be as high as 24 percent of revenues.

6. Mirrlees and others (2011) identify the characteristics of a good tax system for any open high-income economy in the twenty-first century.

7. For example, introduction of the VAT in Ghana in 1995 met with heavy public opposition that led not only to withdrawal of the tax law but also to demand for greater democracy, more inclusive governance, and improved public services. The outcome of the 1996 elections favored the opposition. The new government was able to reintroduce the VAT peacefully in 1998. The importance of tax bargaining was reinforced when, in 1999 and 2003, later governments were able to increase the VAT rate from 10.0 percent to 12.5 percent and then to 15.0 percent through negotiations in which the government committed to use the new tax revenues for publicly popular education and health programs (Osei 2000).

## References

Alm, James, Isabel Sanchez, and Ana De Juan. 1995. "Economic and Non-Economic Factors in Tax Compliance." *Kyklos* 48 (1): 3–18.

Development Committee. 2015. "From Billions to Trillions: Transforming Development Finance Post-2015 Financing for Development: Multilateral Development Finance." Development Committee (Joint Ministerial Committee of the Boards of Governors of the Bank and the Fund on the Transfer of Real Resources to Developing Countries), World Bank, Washington, DC, April 2. http://siteresources.worldbank.org/DEVCOMM INT/Documentation/23659446/DC2015-0002(E)FinancingforDevelopment.pdf.

IMF (International Monetary Fund). 2011. "Revenue Mobilization in Developing Countries." Fiscal Affairs Department, IMF, Washington, DC, March.

Kaldor, Nicholas. 1963. "Will Underdeveloped Countries Learn to Tax?" *Foreign Affairs* 41 (2): 410–19.

Le, Tuan Minh, Blanca Moreno-Dodson, and Nihal Bayraktar. 2009. "Tax Capacity and Tax Effort: Extended Cross-Country Analysis from 1994 to 2009." Policy Research Working Paper 6252, World Bank, Washington, DC.

McArthur, John. 2015. "What Happened at the Addis Financing for Development Conference?" *Brookings Up Front blog*, July 21. http://www.brookings.edu/blogs/up -front/posts/2015/07/20-addis-financing-development-conference-mcarthur# .Va-F28DFf00.

Mirrlees, James, Stuart Adam, Tim Besley, Richard Blundell, Stephen Bond, Robert Chote, Malcolm Gammie, Paul Johnson, Gareth Myles, and James M. Poterba. 2011. *Tax by Design: The Mirrlees Review*. Oxford: Oxford University Press.

Moore, Mick. 2008. "Between Coercion and Contract: Competing Narratives around Taxation and Governance." In *Taxation and State Building in Developing Countries: Capacity and Consent*, edited by Deborah Brautigam, Odd-Helge Fjeldstad, and Mick Moore. Cambridge, U.K.: Cambridge University Press.

OECD (Organisation for Economic Co-operation and Development). 2010. *Citizen-State Relations: Improving Governance through Tax Reform*. Paris: OECD.

Osei, Philip. 2000. "Political Liberalization and the Implementation of Value Added Tax in Ghana." *Journal of Modern African Studies* 38 (2): 255–78.

Tanzi, Vito. 1987. "Quantitative Characteristics of the Tax System of Developing Countries." In *The Theory of Taxation in Developing Countries*, edited by David Newbery and Nicholas Stern. New York: Oxford University Press.

UN (United Nations) General Assembly. 2014. "Report of the Intergovernmental Committee of Experts on Sustainable Development Financing." Report A/69/315, UN General Assembly, New York, August 15. http://www.un.org/ga/search/view _doc.asp?symbol=A/69/315&Lang=E.

World Bank. 2009. *Investment Climate Advisory Services*. Washington, DC: World Bank.

Zucman, Gabriel. 2015. *The Hidden Wealth of Nations: The Scourge of Tax Havens*. Chicago, IL: University of Chicago Press.

## CHAPTER 3

# Tax Policy Reform

This chapter analyzes outstanding issues related to income taxation; natural resource, tobacco, and environmental protection taxation; informal sector taxation; tax incentives and tax expenditures; resource mobilization at the subnational level, including property taxes; and forecasting of tax revenues.

## Equitable Tax Structure: Improving Direct Taxes

Since the 1980s, the value added tax (VAT) has been the workhorse of taxation and has played a major role in increasing the ratio of tax to gross domestic product (GDP) in low- and middle-income countries (LMICs). However, the VAT impinges heavily on the poor and is generally regressive. Part of this problem can be remedied through a pro-poor budget, but broadening and improving direct taxes can also be very effective.

The share of direct taxes in revenue has traditionally been lower in LMICs than in high-income countries (HICs) in the Organisation for Economic Co-operation and Development (OECD). This low share reflects the low per capita income of LMICs, administrative challenges in implementing income taxes, as well as the political hurdles of taxing the rich and local elites. However, it is possible to improve the collection of revenue from direct taxes, both personal and corporate income taxes, in low-income countries (LICs) and lower-middle-income countries, as is evident from figures A.13–A.18 in appendix A. Better revenue collection not only has a positive impact on revenue generation but also improves horizontal equity, augments the visibility of taxes, and increases the demand for higher accountability from government.

In this context, the failure to tax personal incomes of the rich effectively, including the self-employment income of professionals such as doctors and lawyers as well as the investment income of the wealthy, is the most difficult hurdle to overcome. During the 1980s and 1990s, less attention was paid to direct tax reforms due to doubt about whether LMICs had the necessary administrative capacity and political commitment to undertake tax reform. In spite of these challenges, there is an urgent need to put renewed emphasis on the collection of income taxes in LMICs both to mobilize revenue and to enhance the equity of the tax structure.

The main barrier to such an initiative is the absence of political will to tax both ends of the taxpayer spectrum—the rich in society and the poor in the informal sector (Bird and Zolt 2005). However, with greater recognition of the importance of direct taxes for higher revenues, greater equity in taxation, and a growing commitment to collecting taxes from informal agents, it should be possible to broaden the base of income taxes in LMICs.

## Taxation of Exhaustible Natural Resources

Exhaustible natural resources—minerals, oil, and gas—make a significant contribution to GDP, government revenues, and export earnings in more than 20 LMICs. Having a sound tax and revenue policy in place is especially needed in these resource-rich countries.

### Unique Features of This Sector

The natural resource sector has some unique features with regard to tax and revenue. Governments and state authorities in most countries are the legal owners of resources. The marginal revenues from mineral, oil, and gas production far exceed the marginal costs of their extraction; therefore, the difference, which is the resource rent, is significant. Intertemporal exploitation is an important issue for maximizing the net present value of resources in this sector, that is, determining the quantity of resources to extract in each time period.

Most resource-rich LMICs have low capacity for domestic investment and require investment from multinational corporations. While fiscal policy plays an important role in creating an appropriate environment for attracting investment in general, it has added significance for investment in this sector due to the sharing of resource rent. There are two distinct and often opposite viewpoints. On the one hand, foreign investors seek to obtain higher revenues up front and to generate enough cash flow to satisfy lenders that their mining operations will be able to meet repayments. They also prefer to have some sort of fiscal stabilization agreement to reduce future risk arising from possible changes in the fiscal regime.

On the other hand, governments seek to attract more foreign investment while extracting a reasonable share of tax and other revenues up front. When prices are high and surpluses are large, an additional profits tax (progressive income tax or resource rent tax) and graduated royalty payments (a sliding scale or an amount related to earnings or profits) may have to be applied. But when prices are low, mines may realize losses or close down, resulting in both short- and long-term losses for government revenues. Ideally, the tax system should be able to cope with both the ups and the downs of commodity markets. This need for stability is the main challenge for natural resource taxation.

## Corporate Income Tax and Resource Rent Tax

Tax instruments comprise corporate income tax (CIT) and an additional profits tax or resource rent tax, which mandates higher tax rates on profits beyond the normal rate of return. The resource rent tax is attractive in theory, but hard to implement in LMICs, which generally struggle with implementing the CIT effectively, let alone applying a complex resource rent or additional profits tax. A healthy combination of CIT and royalty tax may be the best bet for most LMICs. Some countries choose to apply a higher CIT rate on the natural resource sector, particularly the oil and gas sectors.[1] A relevant issue for CITs is whether mines and oil wells are ring fenced for tax purposes, as the answer has implications for the flow of revenue to the treasury.

## Significant Role of a Royalty

A royalty is the main nontax instrument applied to this sector. While the corporate tax is imposed on income generated in the country, a royalty is the payment to the owner of resources or to the factor of production—land in this case. A royalty can be per unit or ad valorem, is predictable and simple to administer, and offers an assured source of revenue for the treasury. In contrast, income tax revenues are uncertain and often subject to transfer pricing, tax planning, and creative accounting. The royalty rate should be moderate, between 3 and 5 percent on minerals, since high rates of royalty may cause high grading, leaving low-grade minerals. Higher royalty rates are advisable only for high-value minerals like diamonds and platinum (Nakhle 2010). The royalty on oil and gas can be in the range of 5–25 percent but is usually around 10 percent.

Some HICs, such as Norway and the United Kingdom, have gradually eliminated the royalty, while a few countries, such as South Africa, have introduced profit-based royalty. In these cases, the rate of a royalty depends on the operating profits of the company. The experience has not always been satisfactory from the resource country's point of view. In Ghana, for instance, the effective rate of a royalty is based on the profitability of mining operations, determined by computing the operating ratio of a mine during the year. The operating ratio is the ratio of operating margin—total revenue minus operational costs—to total revenue. If the operating ratio is less than 30 percent, then the royalty rate is 3 percent. Operational costs not only include current expenditures incurred by the leaseholder for the purpose of mining, transportation, processing, and sale of minerals, but also incorporate the capital allowances and interest payment for the period. Such provisions in the fiscal regime make it possible for companies to stay below the 30 percent threshold, even during years of high commodity prices and windfall gains to the mining sector—for example, abnormally high gold prices. For instance, no company in Ghana has ever paid more than the 3 percent royalty.

## Stabilization Clause and Windfall Gains

How to capture windfall gains due to an increase in commodity prices is always an issue in the mining, oil, and gas sectors. A sliding scale that links the royalty rate to metal or mineral prices may be applied if provided for in the contract. Investors often ask for a stabilization clause that benefits the company if the tax rate falls and protects it if the rate rises. While this helps to minimize the risk for investors and enables them to make long-term commitments, it also constrains government in times of commodity price booms and limits benefits during periods of windfall gains.

Other types of payments may also be owed to governments, especially in oil- and gas-producing countries. These payments include lump sum bonuses, such as the discovery bonus, lease bonus, and production bonus. Signature bonuses are paid at the time of signing the contract or lease. These bonuses capture some of the anticipated resource values and do not affect the future economic decisions of investors, as payments are up front and mostly one-time occurrences.

Sometimes special royalty rates and income tax provisions are applied to small or artisanal mines. Such means are necessary because indigenous miners operate on low margins and are subject to excessive risks of market fluctuations.

### Incentives for Exploration and Development Costs

Since mining, oil, and gas sectors are highly capital intensive and generally brought in by transnational companies, most countries provide an incentive for exploration and development by allowing accelerated recovery of development costs through tax depreciation, for example, over five years or less. Beyond that, the governments of resource-rich countries should be careful about offering other incentives. Tax incentives generally do not bring additional investments, but they certainly cause loss of revenues.

### A Good Fiscal Regime for the Sector

The following are considered features of a "good" fiscal regime in the mining, oil, and gas sectors in LMICs:

- A CIT in the range of 25–35 percent
- A dividend withholding tax of 15–20 percent
- Royalties (ad valorem) of 2–5 percent on mining and 10–15 percent on oil or gas
- No tariff duty on equipment imports
- A small property tax by local governments
- No export duty on minerals except precious metals
- A normal VAT and zero-rated export tax
- Accelerated and pooled depreciation
- No depletion allowance
- A policy governing ring fencing
- Amortization of exploration costs (5–7 years)
- Ability to expense the costs of environmental protection
- Deductibility of closure costs if a closure fund is established
- Gradual phaseout of tax holidays
- Loss carry-forward rule of 7–10 years.

### *Extractive Industries Transparency Initiative*

To ensure transparency throughout the chain of natural resource exploitation, it is advisable for resource-rich countries to follow the global practices set under the Extractive Industries Transparency Initiative (EITI) standard, which promotes open and accountable management of natural resources. The EITI seeks to strengthen government and company systems, inform public debate, and enhance trust. Crucial to effective implementation is the support of a coalition of government, companies, and civil society.[2]

The EITI emphasizes the principle of "publish what you pay." Natural resources, such as oil, gas, metals, and minerals, belong to a country's citizens. Extraction of these resources can lead to economic growth and social development. However, when poorly managed, extraction too often leads to corruption, conflict, and sometimes even civil war. More openness regarding how a country manages its natural resource wealth is necessary to ensure that these resources benefit all citizens. Under the EITI, information has to be published on each element of the chain, including licensing, contracting, production, tax and royalty payments, and the way revenues flow to the treasury. The EITI report allows citizens to see for themselves how their country's natural resources are being managed and how much revenue they are generating. However, transparency can only lead to accountability if there is public understanding of what the figures mean and public debate about how the country's resource wealth should be managed. Therefore, the EITI standard requires reports to be published regularly, to be comprehensible and transparent, and to promote and contribute actively to public debate.

## "Sin" Taxes and "Green" Taxes: Tobacco and Pollution-Related Taxes

Sin taxes are primarily taxes on cigarettes, alcoholic drinks, sugar-sweetened beverages (in some countries), motoring-related activities (largely taxes on gasoline and diesel fuels), and, to a lesser extent, betting and gambling. Green taxes are primarily excise taxes, such as a tax on carbon dioxide emissions, which is rare in LMICs.

In the case of goods that cause harm, like tobacco and alcohol, and goods that pollute the environment, such as motor fuels, fertilizers, and plastic bags, consumption taxes in the form of excises help to restore the market equilibrium to its optimal level. In the absence of any tax on these products, the market ignores the cost of negative externality and produces beyond the optimal level of quantity, imposing an inefficiency cost on the economy. These taxes not only enhance economic efficiency but also generate more revenues. The challenge is to assess the extent of distortion created by the negative externality and to arrive at the right level of tax. For tobacco, in particular, the price elasticity of demand is quite low, and the tax has to be high to curb consumption, which would yield higher tax revenue, while eroding the tax base as consumers gradually change habits.

Before the Second World War, excises on sin goods were of greater importance in OECD countries than taxes on motoring and pollution, but now the reverse is true. The excise tax rate on gasoline varies greatly across countries. Similarly, taxes on alcohol have become more prominent than taxes on tobacco in LMICs because of a decline in smoking. Again, the tax rate on tobacco and alcohol also varies significantly across OECD countries. In LMICs, tax rates are relatively much lower, and there is large scope for heavily taxing both sin goods and polluting agents.

Environmental taxes have recently received a great deal of traction since the realization that environmental degradation not only is a global threat but also lowers a country's GDP in the medium and long run. For LMICs to achieve sustainable growth and development, tax reform needs to have an element of environmental taxation. Many tax instruments employed by HICs may serve as a model for LMICs.

### Tobacco Taxes

Tobacco taxation is potentially the main policy tool for reducing the severe public health burden of smoking-related diseases; it can also contribute significantly to state revenue collection. Raising taxes on tobacco products is a very cost-effective measure that reduces the consumption of products that lead to premature mortality, while generating substantial domestic revenue for health and other essential social programs (Savedoff and Alwang 2015).

Thus, there is a strong justification for applying high excise taxes to discourage smoking. While nearly all countries tax tobacco products, an excise tax is the most important type of tobacco tax, since it applies uniquely to tobacco products and raises their price relative to that of other goods and services. The tax rate for excises—ad valorem or specific—becomes relevant in this context. Both types of taxes have strengths and weaknesses, but recent country experiences point to the effectiveness of specific taxes. For example, taxes that target the nicotine content of a tobacco product require frequent indexation of the tax rate if there is inflation in the economy, while ad valorem rates may lead smokers to switch to cheaper brands of cigarettes, aggravating the problem.

Most European Union (EU) countries apply a specific excise tax plus an ad valorem excise tax: the specific element in the tax may vary from 5 to 55 percent of the retail price and should be at least 70 euros (€) per 2,000 cigarettes. In the United States, cigarettes are taxed at both the federal and the state levels in addition to any local-level cigarette-specific taxes. As a result, the tax burden in cities like Chicago and New York can be as high as US$7.50 on a pack of 20 cigarettes. The main advantage of higher taxes relates to public health benefits, as many studies worldwide show that higher taxes lead to lower smoking rates, lower public health spending, and, in the medium term, higher labor productivity. Article 6 of the World Health Organization Framework Convention on Tobacco Control, "Price and Tax Measures to Reduce the Demand for Tobacco," recognizes the importance of taxes in reducing the demand for cigarettes.

The share of total excises in retail prices varies between 50 and 68 percent, while the total tax burden on cigarettes inclusive of VAT clusters around 75 percent of the retail price in HICs. No other single product is taxed as highly as cigarettes. Based on experience and the empirical evidence regarding the variety of tax structures applied to tobacco products around the world, the following best practices have emerged with respect to taxing tobacco products (Marquez 2015; WHO 2011):

- Excise taxes should constitute at least 70 percent of final consumer prices.
- Simpler structures are more effective than complex ones, since tiered tax structures are difficult to administer and can undermine the health and revenue impacts of tobacco excise taxes.
- Increases in taxes should exceed increases in consumer prices and incomes in order to reduce the affordability of tobacco products.
- Taxing all brands of cigarettes equally helps to minimize the incentives to switch to cheaper brands.
- Using specific excise taxes enhances the impact of tobacco taxation on public health by reducing the price gap between premium and lower-price alternatives, which limits the opportunities for users to switch to less-expensive brands in response to tax increases. Taxing all tobacco products in a comparable fashion reduces the incentives for substitution.
- Ad valorem taxes are difficult to implement and weaken the impact of tax policy. Since they are levied as a percentage of price, companies have greater opportunities to avoid higher taxes and to preserve or expand the size of their market by manufacturing and selling lower-price brands, which makes government tax revenues more dependent on industry pricing strategies and increases the uncertainty of tobacco tax revenue.
- Specific excise taxes need to be adjusted for inflation to remain effective.
- Tax increases should reduce the affordability of tobacco products. In many countries, where incomes and purchasing power are growing rapidly, large price increases are required to offset growth in real incomes.
- Strong tax administration is critical to minimize tax avoidance and tax evasion, to ensure that higher tobacco taxes lead to higher tobacco product prices and higher tax revenues, and to reduce tobacco use and its negative health consequences.
- Regional agreements on tobacco taxation can be effective in reducing cross-border tax and price differentials and in minimizing opportunities for individual tax avoidance and larger-scale illicit trade.

While only 33 countries impose taxes that constitute more than 75 percent of the retail price of a pack of cigarettes—the taxation level recommended to have an impact on consumption—most LMICs impose extremely low tax rates (WHO 2015). Some do not impose a special tax on tobacco products at all.

### Alcoholic Beverage Taxes

Almost all countries apply excises on alcoholic drinks. Most industrial countries and all EU countries use specific tax rates to target the alcoholic content in beer, still wine, and spirits. Some countries apply a graduated duty on beer depending on the alcohol content. Since 1992, the EU has stipulated minimum excises for alcoholic drinks. For instance, the minimum excise was set at €1.87 per liter of alcohol for beer and at €550.00 per hectoliter of alcohol for spirits. Tax typically accounts for half of the retail price of a drink.

### Automobile and Fuel-Related Taxes

OECD countries impose at least four types of taxes on motoring-related items:

- *Motor vehicles.* An ad valorem tax in most countries and often a luxury tax as an alternative to high VAT
- *Motor fuels.* Mostly ad valorem, but with specific rates in practice and often different rates for gasoline and diesel oil
- *License fees on motor vehicles.* Specific motor vehicle taxes and rates related to vehicle weight
- *Nontax revenues.* Other related taxes, such as driving license fees, road tolls, and parking fees.

All OECD countries, Canada, and the United States levy one or more taxes on motor vehicle fuels, but their rates vary significantly.[3] Historically, taxes on motor fuels were applied primarily to raise revenue, but now significant emphasis is being placed on environmental protection. As regards income distribution among this group of taxes, taxes on vehicles can be progressive, while taxes on fuel and other fees are inherently regressive and impinge heavily on low-income groups. Since the various excises also address environmental issues such as congestion and pollution, the question of whether to tax different kinds of vehicles and fuels differently becomes important.

Most LMICs apply excises on these products, but questions remain about the type of tax—ad valorem or specific—and the level of tax rates. The combined indirect tax rate from VAT and excises should not be above the maximum revenue-yielding rate unless the only objective is to reduce consumption. While demand for tobacco is quite inelastic and can be taxed at very high rates, demand for alcoholic drinks and fuels is not.

### Environment-Related Taxes

The OECD countries employ four broad categories of environmental protection taxes: taxes on road transport; a relatively small group of taxes with a clear-cut environmental rationale, such as taxes on plastic bags and taxes on fertilizers; provisions in the income tax laws (for instance, accelerated depreciation on machinery and equipment) to promote energy saving or control pollution; and a group of charges, fees, and levies that is used mainly to regulate certain environment-related activities.

A wide range of other energy products can also be taxed both for environmental protection and for resource mobilization: use of heavy fuel oil for industrial purposes and use of natural gas, electricity, and coal. Some of these taxes may be inequitable and heavily affect the poor, unless they are well designed and well implemented.

While carbon taxes have been discussed in many countries and used in some EU countries for quite some time, they are a relatively new idea in some LMICs.

## Taxation of Small Businesses

All countries face the problem of taxing micro, small, and medium enterprises (MSMEs), but the size and nature of the problem vary across countries. The share of informal sector in GDP and employment varies between 10 and 20 percent in HICs, but could be as high as 50 percent of GDP and around 90 percent of employment in LMICs. Traders in the informal sector, including not only MSMEs but also larger taxpayers engaged in informal activities, compete unfairly with formal sector businesses, including foreign investors, and this unfair competition can become a major hurdle to economic growth.

### *Considerations of Equity and Cost-Effectiveness*
Two main issues are involved in taxation of informal businesses. First, taxing small businesses is important to promote equity—not generate revenue—and to ensure that normal taxpayers do not hide under the cloak of informality. Taxing them is also important for resource mobilization in the sense that most citizens are willing to pay taxes if others are paying their fair share too.[4] It may be difficult to improve taxation of small businesses as well as enforce local taxes because costs to the government can be very high, including loss of political support, relative to the revenue gains. At the same time, it is important to protect some minimum level of income from taxation. Direct taxation of income is generally difficult to apply to small businesses.

Second, for the sake of cost-effectiveness, the administrative and compliance costs must not exceed revenues. Tax administrations in LMICs are often severely constrained with regard to both resources and skills. They often have to choose between improving the compliance of medium- and large-scale firms already in the tax net, where potential revenue payback is higher, and bringing smaller firms into the tax net, where the potential reward is lower.

### *Problem of Lack of Information*
Taxation is essentially an information game. By definition, informality is weakly documented by the authorities. For normal businesses, the people who have information are owners or shareholders; business managers; third parties such as financiers and bankers; buyers of outputs or suppliers of inputs; external accountants or auditors; or the government regulatory, audit, or service agencies or tax agency. The problem with informality is that information is concentrated in the owner-manager only; most of the other sources of information do not apply to informal business activities.

In HICs, taxpayers may have the capacity to pay taxes but be unwilling to pay them, giving rise to tax avoidance. In LMICs, lack of compliance capacity is an added problem. Even if informal taxpayers are willing to pay taxes, they may lack the necessary skills and means to do so. This requires either exempting businesses, taxing them indirectly, simplifying the tax, or upgrading the compliance capacity of taxpayers. Some of the options for bringing them under the tax net are outlined next.

### Presumptive Taxes

Presumptive taxes—both for income and for consumption, such as the VAT or the goods and services tax—have been used successfully to tax MSMEs. Many countries in Central Asia, such as Kazakhstan, the Kyrgyz Republic, and Tajikistan, have taxed MSMEs for a long time with varying degrees of success. However, once taxpayers are accepted as being below the threshold for presumptive taxes, they tend to stay there. Another approach is to withhold taxes on imports, exports, or purchases made by formal sector private firms and government agencies from unregistered businesses. Many countries already tax inputs. Below an appropriately chosen threshold, modified tax accounting systems for income taxes and a simple turnover tax are also options.

### Administrative Strategies and Incentives

Administrative strategies that focus on MSMEs are also possible; for example, the use of third-party information, improved external audits and investigations, appropriate penalties, and improved education and services for taxpayers may lower compliance costs.

Financial and other positive incentives for moving into the formal sector, such as the provision of institutional finance, may be successfully used. For instance, several studies have found that informal firms in most countries in Africa are well aware of the costs of informality and the potential benefits of becoming formal. Often bureaucratic complexities, not taxation, are the biggest barriers to formalization. The first step is to reduce the costs of formalization and to provide visible benefits of doing so, such as access to banking finances, ability to compete for government contracts, and protection from harassment by local government employees and the police.[5]

If the business registration process and the subsequent regulatory measures could be simplified and tax compliance could be made easier, many informal firms would become formal. In the northern state of Uttar Pradesh in India, for example, small and medium businesses used to be subject to more than 30 annual inspections by a plethora of government departments. A state government reform effort could reduce the number of annual inspections to 24. While more remains to be done, this example highlights the types of reform required for simplification.

### Single Business Permits

Kenya and other countries have experimented with using an annual lump sum tax or a single business permit. The tax is applied to *all* businesses (not just businesses below the VAT threshold): administration of taxes is client oriented and undertaken mostly by local governments, all businesses contribute revenue for public services, and political responsibility and accountability relationships are promoted. The tax rate is scaled to location, market size, sector, and business size (small, medium, and large) using simple criteria such as floor space, number of hotel rooms or beds, and restaurant capacity. It is a highly simplified tax in which all kinds of business license fees are replaced with one annual lump sum tax. The effective tax rate declines with business size so that the actual rate is low for businesses that may also be paying VAT and income taxes.

Having local governments administer informal business taxes is more efficient and cost-effective, as they provide many facilities and services to these businesses. Complementary functions by local governments lower costs and increase effectiveness of identifying, registering, and assessing businesses in the tax base—for instance, business registration; application of land use regulation, including street vendors; property taxation; utility, waste disposal, and other services to business properties; and management of public markets, taxi stands, and bus stations, among others.

The labor costs for local tax officials are also low, making local administration more cost-effective since tax yield per business is low in these cases. In contrast, engaging highly paid professionals of the central revenue authority is more suitable for the taxation of formal businesses.

### Recent Measures to Reduce Cash Transactions

One problem in dealing with informality is the prevalence of cash transactions. To discourage the use of cash and reduce the size of the shadow economy, use of cards at the point of sale may be bolstered through a combination of incentives (for example, lowering the VAT on card transactions) and legal obligations (for example, requiring merchants of a certain size to accept cards). The incentives would lower the operational burden on merchants when they accept cards. For example, the Republic of Korea encourages the use of cards by giving a 2 percent VAT reduction on all card transactions, auditing merchants who refuse to install card terminals, and ensuring that no extra fees are charged at the point of sale. As a result of these measures, the number of point-of-sale card acceptance terminals doubled from 6 million in 1999 to 12 million in 2001, and the government's VAT revenues from card transactions increased to more than €1.7 billion in 2001.

Similarly, Mexico's banks created a fund to provide electronic transaction terminals at relatively low fees to smaller merchants. Mexican regulators helped to increase electronic payments by supporting these initiatives. These efforts multiplied the number of cashless point-of-sale transactions by more than 400 percent between 2002 and 2008. Several countries, including France, Greece, Italy, the Netherlands, Norway, Sweden, and Turkey, have imposed caps on cash payments and require merchants to issue receipts for each transaction. These measures have made fiscal controls easier and allowed merchants to operate more efficiently.

## Tax Incentives and Tax Expenditures

Tax expenditures are the revenue losses from exclusions, exemptions, deductions, tax credits, preferential tax rates, and deferrals. In a way, tax expenditures are very similar to direct spending through the budget. Tax expenditures are measured relative to the normal tax system. The fact or even the general perception that well-connected groups of individuals or companies are receiving preferential treatment under the tax laws severely jeopardizes the integrity and effectiveness of the tax system.

### Major Source of Revenue Leakage

Tax expenditures are a major source of revenue leakage both in LMICs and in HICs. Leakage can run as high as 5–6 percent of GDP even in some OECD countries, including the United Kingdom and the United States.[6] Sometimes governments award tax incentives directly or indirectly through export processing zones (EPZs) in the name of attracting higher investments to the economy. However, some companies take advantage of tax incentives through EPZs, while conducting the bulk of their business outside of such zones. These companies use EPZs as a place for hanging a signboard or as a postal address only. In Ghana, for instance, logging industries were granted EPZ status even though most of their inputs came from Ghana and their operations were wholly domestic (Klemm 2009). Outside of Accra, there is a long, continuous line of one-room industrial units that have no activity but claim to be registered within an EPZ.

Economists have long argued that tax incentives are poor instruments for attracting investments, even in theory, and are highly abused in practice. However, governments argue that they are obliged to give tax incentives because their neighbors are giving them, and there is some truth in this contention (the "race to the bottom"). For instance, Southeast Asian countries are replete with all kinds of tax incentives, and the argument is the same: the Philippines gives incentives because China gives them, Vietnam gives incentives because the Philippines does, Thailand follows the Vietnamese example, and the chain goes on and on. Although there is no systematic way to bring all of these countries around a table and make them agree to a basic norm of providing or not providing tax incentives, some LMICs are now realizing the poor choice they made when granting tax incentives and have started to rationalize and even eliminate them. In addition, some progress is being made in regional harmonization of tax incentives, for example, in East Africa.

### Need for Transparency

Although tax incentives are still widespread in many LMICs, at the very least, there should be transparency around tax expenditures, including those generated by tax incentives. At present, most LICs cannot or simply do not publish a list of recipients or the estimated revenues forgone. This lack of transparency leads to discretionary concessions, backdoor dealings, outright corruption, and other abuses and helps to legalize tax avoidance by well-connected firms. Even if a more detailed and sophisticated analysis of tax expenditures by most LMICs is not feasible, an industry and regional inventory of recipient businesses, with a simple accounting of revenue lost, would go a long way toward improving tax administration and compliance (OECD 2010).

### Including Expenditure Accounts in the Annual Budget

The next step is to publish tax expenditures as a line item in the annual budget so that they receive the same level of scrutiny as direct spending programs through line ministries and government agencies. Including tax expenditures in the budget does not imply any value judgment about their merits or effectiveness. It is primarily meant to increase the transparency of the tax system and to allow the legislature to debate and review the provisions annually and get a sense of the revenue loss involved. The good news is that estimating tax expenditures from direct tax instruments is relatively straightforward and is becoming more prevalent in LMICs. Tax expenditure accounts are now routinely produced, not only by HICs, but also by Latin American countries and some African and Asian countries as well.

The process is time and data intensive at least in the initial years, but, once the database is created and the exercise is undertaken as part of annual budget making, it becomes less arduous. It pays rich dividends in the long run and has the potential to enhance the tax-to-GDP ratio by 2–3 percentage points, depending on the country. Estimating expenditures clearly is vital in the context of domestic resource mobilization, particularly in LICs.

## Special Measures to Deal with Transnational Transactions

Tax evasion by super-rich elites and multinational corporations is facilitated by the existence of offshore financial centers or "tax havens" that often facilitate aggressive and sometimes illegal forms of tax evasion in jurisdictions of low- or no-taxation regimes, weak regulatory systems, and lack of transparency about ownership. Some studies suggest that revenue losses from a single method of transfer pricing may be as high as 5–10 percent of total tax revenues in many LICs (Cobham 2005). These practices clearly undermine the ability of tax authorities to tax wealthy individuals and large firms, with serious consequences both for the equity of tax systems and for resource mobilization. International actors have a particularly important role to play in this policy arena.

### Combatting Base Erosion and Profit-Shifting Practices

Transnational companies employ sophisticated methods of tax planning and profit shifting. Such tax avoidance used to be a major problem for LMICs but has become a matter of concern even for HICs. In a meeting in September 2014, the Group of Twenty (G-20) finance ministers and central bank governors set a goal of increasing GDP by 2 percent by 2018. Such an increase could add more than US$2 trillion to the global economy and create millions of jobs. They are aware of the difficulty of taxing transnational transactions and made a strong commitment to taking "a global response" to cross-border tax avoidance. They endorsed a global common reporting standard for Automatic Exchange of Information (AEOI) and prepared a plan for LMICs to participate in AEOI. They also agreed to finalize the Base Erosion and Profit Shifting (BEPS) Action Plan in 2015 and to engage LMICs as well.[7]

AEOI involves a systematic and regular transmission of taxpayer information regarding different categories of income by the source country to the residence country. It seeks to provide timely information on noncompliance and to reduce multinational tax avoidance and offshore tax evasion in LMICs.[8] The BEPS agenda, in contrast, focuses on reigning in tax-planning strategies of multinationals that exploit gaps in tax laws and rules to shift profits artificially to low- or no-tax jurisdictions where there is little or no economic activity. BEPS aims to furnish tools to ensure that taxes are paid where multinationals actually do business and profits arise. This measure is significant for LMICs, which rely heavily on CIT, primarily from foreign companies and multinational enterprises.

### OECD 15-Point Plan Proposal

The G-20 countries and the OECD have come up with a new set of initiatives to combat this problem. Two years ago, the G-20 countries asked the OECD to suggest reforms that would curb such practices and ensure that multinationals are taxed where economic activities take place and value is created. The OECD released the resulting BEPS proposals—the 15-point action plan—in October 2015, and the G-20 governments approved them in November. These proposals are shaking up the arena of multinational taxation. Companies are now required to do more country-by-country reporting to indicate where they really earn their revenues, hold their assets, and employ people and where they book their profits, detailed information that has traditionally been lacking in their published accounts.

The 15-point plan includes various steps:

- Addressing the tax challenges of the digital economy
- Limiting base erosion involving interest deductions and other financial payments
- Countering harmful tax practices by taking into account transparency and substance more effectively
- Preventing the granting of treaty benefits in inappropriate circumstances
- Preventing the artificial avoidance of permanent establishment status
- Aligning transfer pricing outcomes with value creation
- Measuring and monitoring BEPS
- Imposing mandatory disclosure rules
- Providing guidance on transfer pricing documentation and country-by-country reporting
- Making dispute resolution mechanisms more effective
- Developing a multilateral instrument to modify bilateral tax treaties.

## *A New Paradigm*

These new provisions will give the tax authorities a clearer picture of the extent to which profits are being moved around for tax purposes and the way to hinder such practices. National tax authorities will now receive more information on the tax arrangements that multinationals have with different countries. The European Commission, for instance, has started investigating what are suspected to be unfair deals that Ireland, Luxembourg, and the Netherlands have struck with companies, such as Fiat Chrysler and Starbucks. Also, EU countries have started implementing the OECD recommendations by agreeing on the AEOI regarding their cross-border tax rulings.

Anticipating new regulations requiring greater transparency, some firms are already changing their tax practices to enhance transparency and improve compliance. Amazon, for example, has opened taxable branches in European countries and is no longer diverting its profits to low-tax Luxemburg. The low-tax-rate jurisdictions are also starting to dismantle their tax minimization structures. However, much work remains to be done by the governments involved, as the OECD guidelines are not legally binding and implementation is subject to each country's legislation. In addition, the BEPS Action Plan does not include all international tax issues affecting LMICs. Therefore, implementing and expanding the BEPS Action Plan in LMICs will require additional tax and regulatory reforms, technical assistance, and capacity building.

As the G-20 agenda envisages participation of LMICs in AEOI and the BEPS Action Plan, international aid agencies, particularly the World Bank and the International Monetary Fund, can play a critical role in helping LMICs to clean their tax policy and tax laws and to strengthen their administrative capacity to manage and shape a new model of international taxation.

## Resource Mobilization at the Subnational Government Level

Decentralization is an ongoing international phenomenon that focuses on creating strong local governments. Decentralization helps to improve efficiency in service delivery, enhance political and fiscal accountability, and change the process of entering into a fiscal contract with the government. Local government taxes contribute significantly to the domestic resource mobilization agenda in LICs and, at the same time, support the provision of local services that affect people the most. Since it has the potential to engage taxpayers, decentralization also ensures better use of funds by the local government, as people take more interest in how what they pay locally is spent and in what they can see. However, a lack of an effective property tax, one of the most important subnational taxes, is an important weakness in the tax systems of LMICs. It involves significant revenue losses and adversely affects redistribution of wealth in society, as property is one of the assets owned by richer segments of the population. In addition, an appropriate tax on land can be instrumental in promoting more efficient use of land.

### Devolution of Service Delivery and Local Taxation

Decentralization includes the assignment of service delivery functions and expenditure responsibilities as well as the assignment of revenue: delegation of "function," followed by devolution of "finance." Revenues at the local government level come from own taxes and fees plus fiscal transfers from the central government supplemented by borrowing, debt, and capital finance. To develop own revenues for local government, it is necessary to decompose tax bases vertically between the center and subnational levels and to identify revenue sources with low mobility within the local jurisdiction. Transfers are usually required for correcting regional imbalances.

Local taxes are defined as those that satisfy the following criteria. Local governments can (a) decide whether to levy the tax; (b) determine the precise base of the tax; (c) decide on the tax rate; (d) in the case of "direct" taxes (income taxes), assess the tax imposed on any particular taxpayer, individual, or business; (e) administer the tax; and (f) keep all collections.

### Models of Local Government Taxation

The following types of revenue allocation are available at the subnational level:

- *Independent subnational taxes.* Legislation, administration, and revenue are under the control of regional governments, often under broad guidelines from the central government (property tax).
- *Centrally assisted subnational taxes (co-administration).* Legislation and revenue are directly under the control of regional governments, but the administration could be shared with the central government—for example, property tax with central valuation.
- *Surcharges (piggy-backing).* Administration is under central control, while policy discretion is given to regional governments to set a rate on the nationally determined tax base. Revenue is given back to the regions on the basis of the tax rate, origin of revenues, residence of taxpayers, or some formula—for example, income taxes and VAT in Canada.
- *Tax sharing (transfer).* All policy and administration are under central government control. A portion of revenue is given to regional governments on the basis of origin, residence, or some formula—for example, VAT in China and transitional economies of the former Soviet Union.
- *Revenue sharing (transfers and grants).* All policy, administration, and revenue are under central government control. Revenue can then be given back to the regional governments through revenue sharing based on a formula.

More concretely, some revenue instruments are used at the subnational and local levels:

- *Asset taxes,* including taxes on immovable property (land and building), machinery and equipment, motor and other vehicles (aircrafts, boats, bicycles), and natural resource taxes and charges

- *User charges* for specific services that are rivals in consumption and where exclusion of nonpayers is possible, focusing on the benefit principle
- *Consumption taxes*, including excises, sales taxes, and VAT
- *Income taxes* on individuals (PIT) and businesses (CIT) and payroll taxes on employers.
- *Local business taxes*, including business permit or regulatory fees and licenses.

## Property Taxes

Property taxes can be based on (1) annual rental value, (2) capital value of land and improvements, (3) capital or rental value of land, or (4) land or improvement area. Within these general categories, there are many variations.

The property tax meets the "good tax" argument because it (1) has significant revenue potential; (2) is quite visible, as it is clearly linked to local government services and strengthens public accountability; (3) meets the equity test in terms of ability to pay since assessed value is correlated with the property owners' capacity to pay the tax bill; (4) is less distortive than other local taxes because it is a tax on land and buildings, which are comparatively immobile; and (5) has the potential to be transparent.

### Valuation

There are four basic approaches to determining property value and assessing the tax base:

- *Rental value system.* Many countries (India, Malaysia, Nigeria, and Trinidad and Tobago) use the annual rental value of properties as the tax base.
- *Capital value system.* The capital value system is the main form of property tax base valuation used in OECD countries. The tax base is the market value adjusted by an "assessment ratio."
- *Land value or site value systems.* The tax base is the market value of land, including improvements, such as clearing, grading, and installation of utilities (Australia, Denmark, Estonia, Jamaica, Kenya, New Zealand, and South Africa).
- *Area-based systems.* The area-based systems approach is used in many countries of Central and Eastern Europe as well as in China and Vietnam. Each parcel is taxed at a specific rate per area unit of land and per area unit of structures.

### Tax Rates

Many different tax rate structures are used in LMICs. It is best to choose a simple rate structure that is easy to administer, minimizes cost of administration, and promotes compliance. A good valuation usually addresses differences in ability to pay, so differential tax rates are not necessary for equity reasons and might complicate the administration.

### Authority to Set the Nominal Tax Rate

Sometimes local governments set the property tax rate, sometimes they are only permitted to choose a rate within a prescribed range, and sometimes the rate is set by a higher-level government.

### Exemptions

Four categories of property are generally given exemption: (1) properties that are tax free by international convention, such as foreign embassies, or because they provide a merit good or service; (2) properties of low-income families; (3) "social engineering" or policy exemptions, such as the exemption given to owner-occupied premises, which are meant to encourage homeownership and are politically popular; and (4) properties owned by governments or nonprofits.

The policy of exemptions has the problem of "exemption creep," as in the case of VAT and income taxes.

### Property Tax Administration

The four key components of property tax administration are (1) identifying all properties; (2) keeping the records and updating the tax roll (cadaster); (3) valuing and revaluing properties; and (4) handling tax collections, enforcement, and appeals.

### Property Transfer Taxes

Taxes on property transfers are widely used for immovable property.

### Underutilization of Property Taxes

Property taxes satisfy most of the "good tax" characteristics: they are efficient because they do not distort investment decisions and they fall on those who have the ability to pay. Yet they are underused around the world. This is especially true in LMICs. Low- and lower-middle-income countries, in particular, fail to tax the property sector efficiently, indicating administrative inefficiencies and the underdeveloped state of their economies (see figure A.13 in appendix A).

The main reason for the underutilization of property taxes is the lack of political will and poor administration at the local government level. These taxes fall mostly on well-to-do people who are politically influential and manage to get the tax diluted or neglected. Since local authorities administer the taxes, local elites are able to influence their administration as well. Thus, notwithstanding the fact that the tax is in place, it is generally ineffective.

Valuation is at the core of this tax, and valuation is mostly neglected due to bureaucratic inefficiency and political inertia: even if a property tax is in force, it raises negligible amounts of revenue. As a result, subnational governments often have to depend on central government subventions, especially in LICs. This tax is also not a priority of international organizations, like the OECD, the International Monetary Fund, or the World Bank, which focus predominantly on national taxes.

## User Charges

Recently more emphasis has been placed on user charges because of their dual role in promoting economic efficiency and generating revenue.

User-charge financing is more attractive due to the greater share of benefits accruing to direct users. User charges ideally should be determined using marginal cost pricing; however, in practice some form of average cost pricing may be necessary. Another approach is to use "average incremental cost," which is widely used in aid-funded projects. Exemption from user fees should be an exception and not a rule and should be well justified.

For equity reasons, basic needs services may be free of user charges. Equity concerns may be left for other public policies like tax policy or progressivity of property taxes or, better still, the expenditure route.

## Income and Consumption Taxes (Excises, Sales Tax, or VAT)

Income and consumption taxes are used if more subnational "own-source" revenue is required either to expand the size of subnational activities or to make them more self-sufficient.

Local income taxes are generally levied at a flat rate, are locally determined, and have the same tax base as the national income tax collected by the central government or by the state government, depending on the latter's administrative capability. They are more feasible in HICs; in LMICs, even central governments have trouble collecting revenue from the PIT, so income taxes are less likely to be a major source of revenue for local governments. Similar issues arise with the CIT.

A strong economic and administrative case can be made for regional and even local excises with respect to vehicle-related taxes: fuel tax, toll roads, annual automobile registration, and driver's license fees. Sales tax is common both in HICs and in LMICs. Local governments can apply a sales tax as well or piggyback it on the state or national tax. VAT at subnational levels is quite hard to design, especially in federal structures. Sometimes an origin-based VAT may have to be used.

Subnational business taxes are popular with local governments. They are essentially a production-origin-based VAT applied on income rather than consumption (destination). Business licenses may be an effective method of taxing the informal sector at the local government level, as in Kenya.

## Notes

1. For instance, Vietnam has reduced its CIT rate to 20 percent, but applies a 60 percent corporate tax rate on oil and gas.
2. Launched in 2002 by the U.K. Department for International Development, the EITI is supported by a range of governments in both HICs and LMICs, along with civil society groups. For details, see http://www.DFID.gov.uk and http://www.eitransparency.org/about.htm.

3. For instance, the United Kingdom levies excises of approximately US$1.30 per gallon (roughly 4 liters) of gasoline, while the United States applies only US$0.40.

4. In countries with a large informal sector, the willingness of other citizens to comply is found to be lower (Torgler and Schneider 2007).

5. For discussion, see Kamunyori (2007) and Engelschalk (2004).

6. LeBlanc (2013) presents a comparative picture of tax expenditures in some OECD countries.

7. Communiqué Meeting of G-20 Finance Ministers and Central Bank Governors, Cairns, September 20–21, 2014.

8. See http://www.oecd.org/tax/automatic-exchange/.

## References

Bird, Richard, and Eric Zolt. 2005. "Redistribution via Taxation: The Limited Role of the Personal Income Tax in Developing Countries." International Tax Program Paper 0508, Joseph L. Rotman School of Management, University of Toronto, Toronto.

Cobham, Alexander. 2005. "Tax Evasion, Tax Avoidance, and Development Finance." QEH Working Paper 129, Queen Elizabeth House, Oxford University, Oxford.

Engelschalk, Michael. 2004. "Creating a Favorable Tax Environment for Small Business." In Taxing the Hard-to-Tax: Lessons from Theory and Practice, edited by James Robert Alm, Jorge Martinez-Vazquez, and Sally Wallace, ch. 10. London: Elsevier.

Kamunyori, Sheila. 2007. "A Growing Space for Dialogue: The Case of Street Vending in Nairobi's Central Business District." Department of Urban Studies and Planning, Massachusetts Institute of Technology, Cambridge, MA.

Klemm, Alexander. 2009. "Causes, Benefits, and Risks of Business Tax Incentives." IMF Working Paper Wp/09/21, International Monetary Fund, Washington, DC.

LeBlanc, Pierre. 2013. "Tax Expenditures: An OECD-Wide Perspective." Organisation for Economic Co-operation and Development, Paris. Pierre.leblanc@oecd.org.

Marquez, Patricio V. 2015. "Making the Public Health Case for Tobacco Taxation." Investing in Health, World Bank Group Blog, July 6. http://blogs.worldbank.org/health /making-public-health-case-tobacco-taxation.

Nakhle, Carole. 2010. "Petroleum Fiscal Issues: Evolution and Challenges." In The Taxation of Petroleum and Minerals: Principles, Problems, and Practice, edited by Philip Daniel, Michael Keen, and Charles McPherson, ch. 4. London: Routledge.

OECD (Organisation for Economic Co-operation and Development). 2010. "Tax Reform, Responsiveness, and Accountability." In Citizen-State Relations: Improving Governance through Tax Reform, ch. 2. Paris: OECD.

Savedoff, William D., and Albert Alwang. 2015. "The Single Best Health Policy in the World: Tobacco Taxes." CGD Policy Paper 062, Center for Global Development, Washington, DC. https://www.cgdev.org/publication/single-best-health-policy-world -tobacco-taxes.

Torgler, Benno, and Friedrich Schneider. 2007. "Shadow Economy, Tax Morale, Governance, and Institutional Quality: A Panel Analysis." IZA Discussion Paper 2563, Institute for the Study of Labor, Bonn.

WHO (World Health Organization). 2011. *WHO Technical Manual on Tobacco Tax Administration*. Geneva: WHO. http://apps.who.int/iris/bitstream/10665/44316/1/9789241563994_eng.pdf.

———. 2015. *Report on the Global Tobacco Epidemic, 2015: Raising Taxes on Tobacco*. Geneva: WHO. http://www.who.int/tobacco/global_report/2015/en/.

## CHAPTER 4

# Tax Administration Reform

Several factors are exerting pressure for tax administration reform in low- and middle-income countries (LMICs). First, revenues are needed to enhance economic growth and maintain the quality of public services, and satisfying the demand for higher revenues requires reforming the tax administration. Second, economic growth and structural changes generate more tax revenues, putting further pressure on tax administrations to improve and innovate. Third, globalization and international competition for investment require good governance, and pressure for good governance encourages public sector accountability as well as improved performance, including in the area of revenue administration. As a result, governments worldwide have been undertaking organizational, management, and budget reforms to enhance public sector performance. Over the last two decades, there has been worldwide interest in improving tax administrations, and considerable reforms have taken place. This change has been furthered by the spread of digital information and communication technology (ICT), which has allowed fundamental changes in organizational and business processes.[1]

Traditionally, tax administrations have focused on regulating and enforcing tax laws, paying little attention to taxpayer services. This situation is changing rapidly worldwide, and the new approach is to treat taxpayers as customers. Thus, tax administrations recognize their obligation to offer quality taxpayer services, and the interaction between administrations and taxpayers has become taxpayer focused, easy, convenient, and friendly. This philosophy is behind most of the new initiatives in tax administration reform.

The following are some of the key approaches to improve performance:

- Corporatization (revenue authority)
- Integration of domestic or inland revenues under functional organization
- Client-based organization
- Self-assessment and withholding at source and installment taxes
- Selective or risk-based compliance management

- Effective use of ICT
- Efforts to make the collection process more user friendly and to strengthen taxpayer services
- An overall human resource management (HRM) strategy.

## Corporatization

The basic idea is to make tax administration more businesslike and client oriented rather than stiff, bureaucratic, and distant. International financial institutions and aid agencies have proposed that revenue collection authorities are more effective when they operate with some degree of autonomy at an arm's length from the state and with a commercial focus. They have increasingly concentrated their tax work on creating autonomous revenue authorities (Fjeldstad and Moore 2007).

### Autonomous Revenue Authorities

Autonomous revenue authorities were introduced partly at the initiative and urging of donors and international financial institutions. Most of them were established in environments where corruption and politicization of tax administration were widespread, making this reform highly welcomed. Most of these bodies have been granted some degree of autonomy. The tax administration is partly or fully removed from the direct control of the ministry of finance. Those who administer the authority have some independence to structure and manage it, including the hiring and firing of staff.

This reform often involves a major internal restructuring that may include merging two or more agencies such as customs, income tax, and sales tax into a single agency and recruiting new staff from the old tax administration, the central bank, and the private sector. Employees of the authority are generally not bound by the civil service pay structure and may have better compensation packages and service conditions, helping to maintain higher levels of staff integrity.

### Degree of Autonomy and Interdependence

The question of autonomy is important in this context. Managerial autonomy to run a tax agency on a day-to-day basis in a professional way makes perfect sense, keeping in view its special functions. However, the agency's relationship with the ministry of finance and the level of political control are often problematic. Government revenues are the lifeline of the government, and therefore top management of the revenue authority cannot be completely free or fully autonomous. They should be responsible to someone or, preferably, to some institution—whether the minister of finance, the president, or the legislature through a parliamentary body.

Many tax administrations are inefficient, corrupt, and in need of reform. However, the success of any agency depends on its relationship with other agencies, particularly with the ministry of finance in this case. The revenue authority, while maintaining its autonomy, needs to coordinate with the ministry of finance, especially over tax and budgetary issues.

### Requirement for an Effective Revenue Authority

The effectiveness of revenue authorities is likely to be maximized if (a) an authority has a guaranteed budget that cannot be easily changed by the government in power and can be linked to its performance, for instance, a percentage of revenue collected; (b) its status, responsibilities, and powers are protected by law; (c) appointments to the supervisory board are made by a variety of public agents (for example, different ministries) and nongovernmental agencies (for example, business or lawyers associations); (d) appointments are of fixed duration; (e) managerial responsibility and operational functions are delegated properly to staff at various levels; (f) staff are answerable only to the supervisory board and are free of political interference; (g) the authority exhibits enhanced transparency and accountability; and (h) a system of performance targets based on accrual accounting is used to assess the unit cost of services so that performance can be judged correctly and fairly, as setting targets internally may give rise to moral hazard (for example, as occurred with the Tanzania Revenue Authority).

At the same time, a sustainable organizational autonomy clearly cannot be granted only by legal provisions; it is always under threat and has to be continually earned. Too much protection in the name of autonomy and no engagement with other public institutions like the parliament makes the authority insular and unaccountable.

### Experience of Revenue Authorities

Revenue authorities with varying degrees of autonomy are now common, especially in LMICs. There are two main models:

- A unified semiautonomous body with a formal board or advisory group comprising external officials and nonofficials, including representatives of businesses and taxpayers (for example, in Argentina, Bulgaria, Canada, Mexico, Singapore, and South Africa), often ultimately answerable to the cabinet or the president
- A unified semiautonomous body still accountable to the minister of finance but enjoying considerable independence (for example, in Australia, Chile, Hungary, the Republic of Korea, and Romania).

Revenue authorities have had mixed experiences, and not all have been equally successful. The most successful have been cases where the revenue authority has received strong, stable political support at the highest level (the president or prime minister). Revenue authorities often receive strong, higher-level support in the initial stages, but then support gradually diminishes, as does their performance (for example, in Peru and Uganda).

## Organizational Setup and Management: Integrating Inland Revenues and Functional System

Tax administrations around the world are organized in one of four traditional organizational structures:

1. Type of tax, with separate departments responsible for income tax, value added tax (VAT), excises, and other taxes
2. Functions performed, with departments responsible for assessment, collection of tax arrears, taxpayer audits, and other functions across all types of taxes
3. Type of taxpayer or client, with departments responsible for large enterprises, small or medium enterprises, wage and salary earners, and other taxpayers
4. Combinations of two or more types of the three organizational structures.

The type-of-tax structure is the oldest and can still be found in many countries. Recently, there has been a distinct move toward reorganizing domestic and inland revenues under a functional setup. Instead of having separate directorates of income tax, VAT, goods and services tax, excises, social security taxes, and trade taxes, various departments are integrated under one commissioner or director general and are organized on the basis of functions, such as assessment, collections, audit, and so forth. High-income countries have designed and implemented various combinations of these structures.[2] Each of the four types of structures has advantages and disadvantages, and switching from one structure to another is not without costs.[3]

### Organization by Type of Tax
The long-standing problems associated with type-of-tax administration have been widely analyzed, including by the World Bank. Some of these problems are as follows (KPMG Peat Marwick 1995):

• Duplication of effort, as each department conducts the functions for its own tax, including taxpayer registration, taxpayer services, audits, and compliance
• Fragmentation of resources for enforcement
• Inefficiencies in operations, which adversely affect organizational performance and resources
• Shortcomings in management and staff performance of all departments
• Deficiencies in revenue collection and control of tax evasion, which ultimately lead to lower government revenues
• Lack of coordination and data sharing among departments, which leads to higher tax evasion and avoidance.

Type-of-tax administration also creates significant burdens for taxpayers, including increased time and expenses when they are subjected to multiple registrations, audits, and other interactions with separate tax departments.

## Organization by Function
The functional structure has gradually become more prevalent and successful. This type of tax administration is organized by the type of work performed, as grouping together activities that require similar skills allows specialization in core administrative areas. Most international agencies and tax experts favor this model, which has the following benefits:

- Improved efficiency and effectiveness in collection and audit, as all taxes are covered simultaneously, which makes it possible to conduct fewer but more in-depth field visits, improves the feasibility of cross-checking data and accounts, and saves time
- Use of unified taxpayer identification and accounts (one taxpayer, one set of accounts) and improved collection, making it possible to offset refunds against taxes and penalties
- More efficient identification of taxpayers, because if a firm is registered for one tax, it is registered for all taxes
- Creation of a one-stop shop for taxpayers that lowers the costs of compliance by eliminating duplication, for example, the need for separate audits at different times by different tax officials focused on one tax—for example, income tax or VAT
- Taxpayer segmentation to improve services and the efficiency of enforcement for different client groups
- Standardization of similar processes across all taxes, which helps to improve compliance, for example, by providing one access point for registration, service, and payment
- Simpler procedures for taxpayers
- Greater uniformity across the organization and ability to group all core functions together for better management and control
- Computerization of all work processes
- Greater efficiency and higher productivity of overall tax administration by reducing the duplication of processes
- Early detection of noncompliance and improved compliance by producing a complete view of taxpayer behavior across all types of taxes.

However, there are disadvantages as well:

- Need for a higher level of training for officers (multitax versus single-tax specialization)
- Limited organizational development, especially at higher levels, as officers become specialized in one function and are not capable of managing the overall tax system.

Functional structures are used extensively in most high-income countries (HICs) and are becoming more common in LMICs as well. A study by the Organisation for Economic Co-operation and Development (OECD) Forum on Tax Administration found substantial reliance on the functional model of organization—13 of 49 revenue agencies reported having adopted the functional model as the primary criterion for structuring their tax administration, while 30 other revenue bodies reported using a broad mix of criteria, including the functional one. Thus, 43 of 49 tax administrations employ some level of functional organization (OECD 2011).

Countries that rely exclusively on taxpayer segmentation (by large, medium, and small taxpayers) also organize taxpayer segments, like large taxpayer offices, under a functional structure, with components for audit, collection, and taxpayer services.

### Organization by Type of Taxpayer or Client

The main rationale for organizing tax administration by type of taxpayer or segment is that different taxpayer groups have different characteristics, tax compliance behavior, and levels of risk for revenue loss. Small taxpayers may be willing to pay but lack the capacity to do so. They have high costs of compliance and find it difficult to self-assess their tax liability. Large taxpayers may have the capacity to pay but be unwilling to pay. They deserve special attention because they pay most of the tax revenues in any country. On average, the largest 10 percent of taxpayers pay 90 percent of tax collected and the largest 1 percent pay 50 percent of tax collected. Their costs of compliance are low, but they have the capacity to engage in tax planning and creative accounting; if they have multinational or multibusiness operations, they also have the capacity to use abusive transfer pricing. Other categories of taxpayers include high-wealth individuals, pay-as-you-earn (PAYE) individuals (employees), tax-exempt organizations or nongovernmental organizations, microbusinesses, and informal sector firms. Each major type of taxpayer may need a specialized package of services to reduce compliance costs and enhance compliance. This need has led to a shift from an integrated function to a client-based structure.

This client-focused structure has both advantages and disadvantages. The main advantages include the following:

- Close monitoring of large taxpayers, which improves compliance overall
- Ability to conduct frequent all-tax audits using highly capable auditors and joint audits, which ensures consistency between accounts—VAT, excise, income tax, PAYE, social security contributions, and possibly customs
- Maintenance of detailed accounts in computer systems, which assists with tax analysis modeling and revenue forecasting
- Creation of large taxpayer units offering a one-stop shop, including tax interpretations and advance rulings
- For small and micro taxpayers, ability to focus on active registration and presumptive tax collections, which calls for different types of skills and training than those for monitoring of large taxpayers
- Appointment of a dedicated management team to oversee all compliance and service operations of each unique taxpayer segment

- Feasibility of better research and understanding of compliance issues of each taxpayer segment and ability to develop and implement compliance strategies unique to each segment, such as more targeted audits
- Improved service provision and targeted taxpayer education
- Better management of risk levels unique to each group and allocation of resources commensurate with the risk level of each taxpayer segment.

However, this model also has disadvantages:

- Higher administrative costs because common core and support functions, like ICT, are duplicated across taxpayer segments
- Duplication and fragmentation of staff, which may limit the ability to apply the best practice of having centralized staffing
- Inconsistent application of tax laws, policies, and procedures across different taxpayer segments, especially if monitoring and direction from tax administration headquarters are insufficient.

Large taxpayers are an existing, identified tax base. However, focusing too much on one segment raises several questions: Is this base growing? Which potential tax bases in the economy are growing, and which are not growing? What tax bases are being ignored? Where should incremental tax administration effort be spent to yield the highest revenue?

Today functional organizational structures, with partial segmentation of large taxpayers, are the most common arrangement, but some countries have begun to establish medium taxpayer offices and to segment taxpayers who account for 10–15 percent of tax revenues. The U.S. Internal Revenue Service Large and Mid-Size Business Division, established in 1999, is an example of segmentation based on this model.

### Costs of Making the Transition
Concentrating resources on large taxpayer units entails opportunity costs and raises several practical problems. For countries with tax-type administration but no functional organization, the transition poses a major legal and organizational problem. Should the tax administration switch to functional organization before setting up a large taxpayer unit? With limited human resources, is this the most cost-effective use of best and capable personnel? Would other taxes have higher yield or be more cost-effective, such as PAYE and payroll taxes, customs, and withholding taxes?

The main barrier to this transition is the need to change laws; manage the traditional, existing power relationships within the tax administration; and address the challenges of human capacity development, including choosing between multitax training and tax-type specialization or between a team and multifunctional individuals and deciding whether to reengineer complete systems (office systems, computer systems).

The advantages seem to outweigh the disadvantages and the costs. Tax administrations in LMICs should strive to employ a functional organizational structure or at least an organizational structure that is a blend of functional and type-of-taxpayer divisions, as this change is more likely to enhance revenue mobilization.

### Should Customs and Tax Administration Merge?

The reorganization of tax departments in LMICs, particularly the establishment of a revenue authority, gives rise to the question of whether the tax administration and customs should be combined or remain separate. This question is most relevant for LMICs that rely heavily on customs duties, the VAT, and excises collected on imports.

The functions and responsibilities of customs have some basic peculiarities and may resemble those of a police department or a paramilitary organization in some respects. Even in merged bodies with customs and tax administration under a single director general, the two generally conduct their operations more or less independently for a variety of reasons:

- The two agencies have unique and dissimilar processes and procedures.
- Their historical and functional bases are different.
- Their skills and processes are different: while tax administration operates retrospectively, customs operates in real time on matters of border control and revenue collection on traded goods.
- Customs is also concerned about national health, security, and safety.
- ICT is usually developed separately because each agency has different needs.
- In some cases, the two agencies have different levels and rates of modernization, including risk and strategic planning and information technology (IT).

Many LMICs with established revenue agencies have chosen to concentrate solely on strengthening internal tax administration—mainly income taxes, VAT, and excises—and have not incorporated customs operations into the revenue agency. As of 2015, 13 OECD member countries align tax and customs operations within a single agency or directorate, while 21 countries maintain separate bodies (OECD 2015). In the Asia-Pacific region, none of the 22 revenue bodies surveyed by the Asian Development Bank in 2014 has a customs administration function (ADB 2014). Evidently the most common international practice is to keep the two agencies separate. However, the need for ongoing cooperation, close coordination, and exchange of information between tax administration and customs is of paramount importance to the work of both agencies.

### Selective or Risk-Based Compliance Management

Domestic resource management (DRM) entails selective or risk-based compliance management by broadening the scope and effectiveness of audit and strengthening compliance monitoring. Since most governments have switched to self-assessment for all types of taxes, full compliance monitoring and effective audits require selective targeting of taxpayers (Lethbridge 2013). In addition to other compliance management measures, risk-based audit renders the selection more accurate and less arbitrary.

## Audit Plan

The audit division at tax administration headquarters is normally responsible for setting the policy and target for classifying types of audits. Historical data and experience are used to separate the relative risks of the various sizes and classifications of tax-paying entities. Many tax administrations take advantage of the well-used 80/20 principle (20 percent of taxpayers pay 80 percent of tax collected), which excludes the top 20 percent of the highest-turnover taxpayers from any plan or risk selection program and monitors them individually. While this policy has many advantages, it should not be carried out at the cost of omitting high-risk, lower-turnover taxpayers.

The annual audit plan may include input from various sources:

- Previous experience and area-specific knowledge from auditors (knowledge of large taxpayers or specific industries)
- Historical data on actual compliance, trends, and impacts of enforcement to update risk weights and select audit cases yielding the maximum revenue
- Overall taxpayer classification (size, industry type, other)
- Type of business (industrial, commercial, professional, construction)
- Outcomes from the previous years' audit plan
- Estimates of potential revenue per return
- Third-party information, including withholding at source where feasible
- Intelligence gathering
- Risk weighting for random selection within an audit strategy using econometric techniques
- Application of risk-based selection.

## Risk-Based Audit

The audit division should develop a system for identifying the most risky returns or noncompliant taxpayers. Since it is impossible to control and check every single taxpayer, risk management is an important element of an effective and efficient audit program. The number of audits that tax authorities can complete in a given year depends on the number of audit staff, methodology, and processes; generally a small percentage of taxpayers can be audited each year. However, with proper selection, the division should cover up to 90 percent of revenues and provide for a sufficient number of audits to deter noncompliance. At the same time, it is unnecessary to waste scarce enforcement resources in routinely examining low-risk, compliant taxpayers. The audit program should allocate resources to areas that have the most potential for generating additional revenue.

Generally, tax administrations use methods that select high-risk taxpayers for audits. This targeted approach to audits may result in higher revenue than an unstructured approach. To select taxpayers for audit, tax administrations use risk-based criteria that measure a taxpayer's compliance through elements that can be measured in tax returns and the relevant time frame. Various risk criteria can be used and combined into a risk-scoring algorithm, a yardstick that can quantify and compute risk for each taxpayer. A sophisticated risk system may also include criteria for comparisons with industry averages and norms, such as margins, markups, profitability ratios, and matching of third-party data. The main goal of the risk-scoring algorithm is to identify taxpayers with the highest risk to revenues and the highest probability that the audit will discover additional liability.

The risk-based audit selection system is not possible without computerization, if risk is to be calculated for all taxpayers. Unfortunately, many LMIC tax administrations do not have either electronic information from tax returns or historical information over multiple years to do more than a very simple risk analysis. Conducting a simple risk analysis using computers is much better than trying to audit all returns or to identify the riskiest taxpayers manually. The efficiency of a computerized risk-based selection system depends on the availability of inputs, the relevance of the risk criteria, and the quality of the scoring and ranking methods used.

Thus, selection of the criteria and their continuous adjustment are very important. An audit monitoring system is also needed. The selection program should be run on a regular basis during the tax year, as doing so ensures that all tax filers are included and yields more accurate outcomes.

With the use of a risk-based audit selection system, taxpayers can also be satisfied that they are being audited through a procedure that is fully computerized and governed by a fair and automatic process that selects cases without any bias.

## Information and Communication Technology

Tax administration is essentially a business of information management.[4] Modern tax administration is based on the assessment of tax liability, a collection mechanism that includes enforcement as well as enhanced voluntary compliance, effective taxpayer services with a focus on the taxpayer as a customer, effective audit and dispute resolution, and informed decision and policy making. These elements are strongly supported by the use of ICT. Today the use of ICT is not a choice; it is a necessity. For LMICs, its importance in DRM cannot be overemphasized.

### Promoting Transparency and Reducing Corruption
Corruption in taxation is a major issue in many LMICs and clearly affects government revenues adversely. Using ICT in tax administration promotes transparency and reduces the need for face-to-face interaction between taxpayers and tax officials. It therefore has potential to reduce malpractice and corruption in administration, improve taxpayer compliance, and thus enhance DRM.

### Implementing ICT
ICT enables tax administrations to gather and analyze information better and promotes cooperative engagement with taxpayers. It has become increasingly

important, and, according to an OECD estimate, tax administrations now spend at least 15 percent of their total budget on ICT. However, tax administrations in need of ICT systems, particularly in LMICs, face increasingly complex IT-related issues such as prioritization of potential interventions, choice of approach to implementation, and choice of vendor.

Adopting ICT is not a simple matter of arranging funding, buying computers, choosing appropriate software, and employing a few technical experts to computerize the data. Basically, it involves reengineering the entire business model and processes. It is very important for the tax administration to plan and visualize new ways of conducting its business before adopting ICT.

### Using ICT in All Tax Administration Functions

The most prevalent use of ICT systems in tax administration is to strengthen the core tasks of processing returns and payments and collecting relevant information. ICT enables tax administrations to move away from heavy manual processing and to direct their resources to facilitating, monitoring, and enforcing compliance. It provides vital support for risk management, improves the recovery of arrears and tax debt, supports intelligence and fraud detection, and helps to forecast revenue and identify tax gaps. Modern ICT systems support the tax administration's audit and collection functions by gathering and managing information, particularly in areas where noncompliance poses the greatest risk to revenues. In addition, the management information system facilitates decision making by getting the right information to managers and staff.

### Facilitating Taxpayer Compliance

ICT also facilitates voluntary compliance by opening an interactive electronic channel with taxpayers, commonly known as the e-tax system, that includes support for electronic registration, filing, payment, information dissemination, and other functions. Computers plus the Internet expand computing power to all taxpayers and allow for a two-way transfer of data. ICT also offers a powerful means to enhance taxpayer services and education through e-forms and documents, including e-returns, e-filing, e-payment, e-invoices, e-transportation of documents, e-mails, e-videos, chats, and social media. With third-party information and withholding, tax administration can revert from self-assessment to agency assessment or prefilled returns for most taxpayers (except the self-employed). California in the United States has started executing these measures to some extent.

The following are some key guidelines and benchmarks for implementing a successful ICT system:

- *Use ICT to transform tax administration.* The use of appropriate ICT helps tax administrations to become more effective in all aspects of their operations and to maximize the use of scarce resources.
- *Simplify and reengineer processes.* A basic ICT solution should cover the core processes of a tax administration. It also should support sound and

streamlined processes, which implies that process reengineering and best practices must be aligned with the ICT system. There is no benefit in implementing ICT to support outdated and ineffective processes. Before introduction of ICT, the entire tax administration process has to be streamlined and redesigned.

- *Sequence IT improvements.* The use of ICT evolves alongside tax administration practices. In initial stages, tax administrations focus on registering and capturing taxpayer information and filings. Later, audit and case management functions become important: information can be collected from different sources to support the audit function, tax administrations evolve to focus on risk management, and information is used to implement sophisticated risk profiles and select cases for audit. ICT supports the entire sequence of tax administration.
- *Develop a strategy for implementing ICT.* Developing and implementing a coherent ICT strategy is crucial for successful ICT implementation. Sometimes changes in legislation are necessary, organizational structures have to be redefined, and new procedures have to be developed.
- *Use ICT to maintain a service orientation.* Transforming the tax organization into a service-oriented entity is often a time-consuming process that ICT can help to sustain.

In a nutshell, ICT provides technological support to virtually all functions of tax administration: processing registration filings and issuing taxpayer identification numbers, validating and processing returns and payments received through different channels, maintaining taxpayers' accounts, providing tools to identify and pursue delinquent taxpayers, automating appeals tracking, and providing taxpayer service staff with access to taxpayer information to enable a higher level of service. It has become the backbone of modern tax administration and provides valuable tools for improving both enforcement and compliance by enhancing taxpayer education and services. ICT can therefore play an important role in achieving higher DRM, both in LMICs and in HICs.

## Taxpayer Services, Public Awareness, Transparency, and Civil Society Engagement

To mobilize more revenues, strengthen the tax administration, and increase enforcement, it is crucial to improve compliance. For citizens to comply voluntarily, they should not only be aware of the basis on which they are paying taxes but also understand the country's system of taxes, budgets, and expenditures. While it may be difficult to prove a direct link between compliance and taxpayer services, taxpayer services are vital to increasing compliance and therefore to raising domestic revenues.[5] Thus, greater transparency and improved taxpayer services are likely to lead to substantial improvements in compliance by enhancing the perceived legitimacy of the system and creating visible links between taxes and public services. The public generally demands greater tax transparency in almost every country.[6]

Unfortunately, transparency about what taxes are collected and how the money is used is lacking in most low-income countries. As a result, trust in tax administration and government is very low. To strengthen governance and enhance revenues, the tax agenda needs to improve transparency, improve taxpayer services, report tax collections regularly and clearly through the budget, and use some tax earmarking to demonstrate links between tax and expenditure.

### Promoting Voluntary Compliance

The international trend in tax administration is to encourage taxpayers to self-assess their tax liability and then pay the amount of tax to the government. This is a sound approach because the taxpayer has better information on his or her sources of income and it is expensive for the government to assess every taxpayer's return. However, self-assessment only works if taxpayers know their obligations and are able to comply with them. Compliance is better if the costs borne by taxpayers in carrying out self-assessment are low. Thus, an essential element of tax compliance is helping taxpayers to understand their tax obligations and promoting the voluntary and accurate reporting of tax liabilities.

Taxpayer service therefore plays a critical role in maximizing voluntary compliance by providing taxpayers with the information and assistance they need to meet their tax obligations. By using public information, forms, and services effectively and showing taxpayers that they can comply with relative ease, taxpayer services can encourage greater compliance and mobilize higher revenues. An effective taxpayer services strategy integrates three broad ideas:[7]

- *Tax simplification.* Simplified policies and procedures greatly facilitate voluntary compliance.
- *Taxpayer assistance.* Assistance primarily means providing information to help taxpayers to prepare tax returns, resolve issues of filing, and answer any questions that might arise.
- *Facilitation of taxpayer transactions and interactions.* A convenient mechanism, such as e-filing and e-payment, facilitates access to information or to one's account.

### Organizing Taxpayer Services

Although each employee within the organization is responsible for providing effective taxpayer services, it is helpful to establish a dedicated unit responsible for programs, planning, and coordination of initiatives related to taxpayer services at the headquarters and operational office levels. This type of unit may have various titles, including Taxpayer Services Directorate (Costa Rica), Stakeholder Partnerships, Education, and Communication (United States), and Service and Collection (Mexico). The main focus should be on three activities:

1. *Registration or walk-in.* To assist those taxpayers who want to resolve their issues face-to-face. This assistance includes answering taxpayer questions, furnishing tax forms and publications, and helping to prepare tax returns.
2. *Taxpayer education or outreach.* To develop and provide suitable communications and educational products to employees, taxpayers, and other stakeholders,

including practitioners and industry groups, and to deliver them via a variety of channels, including face-to-face, online, by telephone, and in written form. This activity develops forms and publications and updates them regularly on the basis of changes in laws and procedures.

3. *Call center.* To address telephone inquiries in a user-friendly manner. Supported by modern telephone technology, call centers can be an important element in service delivery.

### Providing Self-Service Channels

The international trend in taxpayer service delivery is to provide more consistent advice and to maximize resources through the use of self-service channels (online services or telephone interactive tax assistance). These services direct taxpayers through a series of prompts for a range of services, including e-filing, registration, and accounts balance.

Two other measures are particularly effective in providing better taxpayer services and augmenting the public image of the tax administration: (1) supervising tax officials in order to reduce any arbitrary behavior on their part and (2) creating a partnership between the tax authority and civil society by engaging the community in tax collection efforts.

### Using Taxpayer Services to Build a Positive Image

Taxpayer services staff interact the most with the general public. They are, in effect, the public face of the tax administration. They should have good interpersonal skills and be knowledgeable about laws and procedures. Such skills and knowledge not only help to generate revenue but also create a better public image and foster a more favorable perception of the tax agency.

### Clarifying the Link between Taxation and Public Expenditure

Earmarking tax revenues may be helpful in showing the direct link between tax and expenditure and in enhancing voluntary compliance. Tax earmarking refers to the act of legally committing specific tax revenues to specific expenditures. The most explicit form of earmarking is benefit taxation: charging for a particular service in order to provide that same service. For example, many countries in Africa earmark road taxes collected from fuel sales for road maintenance. In practice, most countries use earmarking to some degree. However, fiscal experts generally do not favor this practice, as earmarking reduces budgetary flexibility in the long term. An example of successful earmarking is the recent increase in the VAT rate in Ghana from 10 percent to 15 percent, with an explicit commitment to spend the resulting revenues on the Ghana Education Fund and Health Insurance Fund.

Strengthening the link between tax revenues and expenditures can be achieved only when earmarking is implemented effectively and transparently.

### Constructive Civil Society Engagement and Partnership on Tax Issues

Civil society engagement is a crucial piece of the relationship between the tax administration and civil society. In principle, business associations should be one of the most important voices arguing for a better tax system and for citizen engagement. Unfortunately, business associations tend to be relatively weak and highly fragmented in LMICs. An interesting possibility is to support the creation of associations of small and medium enterprises as a means of bringing the informal sector into the tax fold. However, large firms control most major business associations. While many countries have smaller business associations, these associations are generally quite weak and poorly resourced.

Taxpayer associations developed on the pattern of business associations have the potential to engage constructively with the government. They can create pressure for greater equity in tax reform and be valuable partners in expanding public education and awareness and building trust in the tax administration. One example, from Sub-Saharan Africa, is the National Taxpayers Association in Kenya, which was formed in 2007. The initiative enjoyed the informal support of the Kenya Revenue Authority, which supported the association as part of efforts to increase taxpayer education and awareness.

This kind of partnership between the tax administration and civil society can support a more equitable and effective tax agenda. Trusted nongovernmental bodies may also reinforce the importance of paying taxes and explain controversial tax issues, increasing confidence in the system through greater understanding. One possible strategy is to work closely with local private sector associations, which, although weak, can serve as a conduit for information and discussion. Outside of government, tax professionals, both accountants and tax lawyers, can work with private firms for tax-filing purposes and serve as a general resource for taxpayers. Tax professionals already play an important role in improving compliance in HICs.

## Behavioral Design of Tax Administration Procedures

The main task of tax administrations is to ensure compliance with tax laws and improve revenue collections, while providing customer services to taxpayers. In order to do this, tax administrations employ a wide range of compliance and customer service programs that aim to change taxpayers' behavior. Many successful development programs rely on people to behave in a specific way, and behavioral economics is helpful for understanding people's behavior.

### Understanding Taxpayer Behavior

The behavioral design of tax administration instruments focuses on developing a better understanding of taxpayers' behavior and attitudes toward taxation—specifically, understanding why taxpayers are compliant or not.[8] Such an understanding can offer helpful clues for developing better and more effective tools to enhance compliance. Behavioral design is both effective and less costly than risk-based audits, which also seek to influence people's behavior.

The standard model of tax compliance assumes that a rational taxpayer assesses the costs and benefits of evading taxes. If the expected net benefits of saving on taxes are higher than the costs—the probability of being caught and the resulting penalties—then the taxpayer will evade taxes. However, factors beyond punitive deterrence also influence taxpayers and their attitude to taxation. Simply increasing the level of deterrence does not guarantee enhanced compliance and often proves to be an expensive tool both for the administration and for the taxpayer. This section discusses some of these factors and alternative approaches to influencing taxpayers and improving their behavior.

### Effect of Norms on Taxpayer Behavior

An individual's behavior is shaped by the widespread desire to "do the right thing." This desire should enhance compliance, as taxpayers will generally comply if they believe that doing so is the right thing rather than if they fear punishment for noncompliance (Wenzel 2005). This desire to comply is linked to both personal norms of the individual taxpayer as well as prevailing social norms. Campaigns to increase taxpayer awareness and taxpayer education primarily target personal norms.

Social norms exert a strong influence on the behavior and choices of individuals. Social norms are more effective if tax evasion is perceived as an exception and if compliance is seen as the norm. If noncompliance is the norm and tax evasion is tolerated in society, people tend to be noncompliant. This is where the image of the tax administration plays an important role: the administration needs to be perceived as fair and trustworthy.

### Fairness and Trust in Tax Administration

Trust, legitimacy, and authority are linked to perceived fairness. OECD (2010) addresses three types of fairness in taxation:

- *Distributive fairness*, which means that government spends revenues wisely
- *Procedural fairness*, which means that the tax administration deals fairly with taxpayers
- *Retributive fairness*, which means that the tax administration applies punishments fairly in case of violation of law and rules.

Compliance improves when taxpayers believe that the tax administration is fair in applying the laws and procedures and in meting out penalties. Transparency and an orientation toward taxpayer service—not just policy—generate trust in tax administration.

### Complexity as a Deterrence to Compliance

Research and experience have shown that people find it hard to make difficult decisions and, when faced with a large number of complex options, tend to choose the default option, which may not be optimal. To most people, taxation appears to be a complex subject, and reducing complexity is likely to improve compliance. The excessive need to use accountants and lawyers in tax matters indicates that the tax system is too complex. One simple way to make it easier to comply is to use plain language, simple forms, and simpler tax laws, where possible. Another is to engage tax accountants in improving communication and compliance. Working with accountants and tax agents helps to garner support for changes in the tax system and improve compliance.

### Broader Role of Government and Economic Factors
Several factors are not under the control of the tax administration but do affect compliance and tax collections, such as economic booms and downturns. During downturns, the tax administration could modify the payment of taxes for small businesses facing liquidity issues.

### Knowledge of Compliance Characteristics
Research has shown that age, gender, education, sector, employment, and income-related factors influence taxpayer behavior (Andreoni, Erard, and Feinstein 1998; Boame 2009). International experience of HICs such as Australia, Sweden, the United Kingdom, and the United States shows the efficacy of changing taxpayer behavior to enhance compliance. The main types of information useful in this regard are related to audit and penalty, taxpayer assistance, and education and social norms.

### Lessons from Behavioral Science for Reducing Fraud, Errors, and Liabilities
The Behavioral Insights Team of the U.K. Cabinet Office has developed seven insights based on behavioral science for improving people's behavior toward fraud, errors, and unpaid liabilities that may help to improve tax compliance.[9] In the United Kingdom, fraud, error, and overdue debt to the government may cost about €40 billion annually.

#### Make It Easy
Make it as straightforward as possible for people to pay tax or debts—for example, prepopulating a form with information improves the accuracy of taxpayer submission. The Internal Revenue Service in the United States has developed a smartphone application that allows taxpayers to check the status of their refund, while the Australian Taxation Office has developed an easy-to-use tax calculator.

#### Highlight Key Messages
Draw people's attention to important information or required actions by, for example, highlighting them up front in a letter or on a website. Drawing people's attention to the most relevant information, particularly about action that is required, seems obvious, but it pays to highlight key messages. People may pay more attention to the first page of a letter than to the back pages, and putting key messages on the envelope itself may be very effective.

#### Use Personal Language
Personalize language so that people understand why a message or process is relevant to them. A great deal of communication from government bodies,

particularly regarding taxes and benefits, is mass-mailed and generic in nature. New technologies make it easy to personalize messages at lower costs.

### Prompt Honesty at Key Moments
Prompt people to be honest at key moments when filling in a form or answering questions. Most people have an inherent desire to be honest, so reminding them of their honesty may be helpful—for example, have taxpayers sign their tax form at the beginning rather than at the end of the process.

### Tell People What Others Are Doing
Highlight the positive behavior of others, for instance, inform taxpayers that "9 of 10 people pay their tax on time." Most people do not commit fraud and believe in paying their liabilities because a strong sense of obligation and fairness is shared widely in the society. Trials using social norms have been found to be quite effective in encouraging tax compliance in Minnesota in the United States as well as in Australia (Bobek, Roberts, and Sweeney 2007; Coleman 2007).

### Reward Desired Behavior
Incentivize or reward behavior that saves time or money. In some cases, it may be possible to find cost-effective ways to motivate individuals by appreciating or rewarding their actions through a simple thank-you note. Also, prizes by lottery can be used to encourage people to file returns or pay taxes. The Chinese government prints lottery numbers on the back of tax-filing receipts. However, care should be taken not to overuse the reward system, as doing so may crowd out an individual's positive motivations.

### Highlight the Risk and Impact of Dishonesty
Emphasize the impact of fraud or late payment, as well as the risk of audit and the consequences for those caught. The risks and consequences of being delinquent and dishonest are not always clear to the person concerned. Warnings and punishments need to be seen as effective, which can be done by highlighting recent successful prosecutions.

### Summary of Lessons from Behavior Science
These insights are known and practiced in HICs. They provide a good checklist for LMICs, particularly those seeking to improve the mobilization of domestic resources.

## Tax Administration Diagnostic Assessment Tool

The Tax Administration Diagnostic Assessment Tool (TADAT) is useful for assessing the strengths and weaknesses of the key components of a country's tax administration system and its level of robustness in the context of international best practices. It highlights those issues that may be addressed with a mix of policy and administrative measures. At the international level, it facilitates an overall view of the condition of tax administration among all stakeholders—country authorities, donor countries, international organizations, and providers of technical assistance. The findings of a TADAT analysis help to set the agenda for improving the tax administration and its implementation. TADAT is supported by the World Bank Group; International Monetary Fund; U.K. Department for International Development; and governments of several countries, including Japan, the Netherlands, and Switzerland.

## Scope and Coverage

TADAT assesses the administration of major direct and indirect taxes critical to central government revenues—corporate income tax (CIT), personal income tax (PIT), VAT, and social security contributions. Presently, TADAT is not designed to assess either special taxes, such as natural resource taxes, or customs administration. The World Customs Organization has developed a parallel diagnostic process for customs.

TADAT assesses the performance of a country's tax administration system with reference to nine performance outcome areas (POAs):

1. *Integrity of the registered taxpayer base.* Registration of taxpayers and maintenance of a complete and accurate taxpayer database
2. *Management of risks to the tax system.* Compliance with tax laws, awareness of compliance risks, and corrective action to mitigate the effects of risks
3. *Taxpayer support to improve compliance.* Information and support to enable taxpayers to comply voluntarily
4. *On-time filing of tax returns.* Timely filing of tax returns, which is the principal means by which a taxpayer's tax liability is determined and becomes due and payable
5. *On-time payment of taxes.* Extent of nonpayment and late payment of taxes, as collection of tax arrears is costly and time-consuming
6. *Accuracy of information reported in tax returns.* Information about the completeness and accuracy of tax returns, as audit and other methods of verification, along with taxpayer assistance, promote accurate reporting and mitigate fraud
7. *Adequacy of dispute resolution processes.* Independent and accessible review mechanisms, which safeguard a taxpayer's right to appeal and receive a fair hearing in a timely manner
8. *Efficiency and effectiveness of operations.* Accounting for tax revenue collections and monitoring them against budget expectations and revenue forecasting, which ensures prompt payment of legitimate tax refunds
9. *Accountability and transparency.* Being answerable for the use of public resources and the exercise of authority and being openly accountable for administrative actions to the finance ministry, the parliament, and the community in general, which build community confidence and trust.

### *Indicators and Measurement Dimensions for the Nine POAs*

TADAT assesses a set of 28 indicators that are critical to tax administration performance and linked to the nine POAs. These indicators are scored and reported on; some have a single dimension, while others have multiple dimensions. Thus, 51 measurement dimensions are taken into account in arriving at the scores for all of the POAs. Each indicator has between 1 and 4 measurement dimensions. To the extent possible, the indicators are oriented toward assessing performance outcomes or results. However, in several cases outputs are used as a proxy for outcomes because tax administrations usually generate performance data on outputs rather than on outcomes and impacts.

As far as possible, TADAT avoids measuring inputs and enabling factors that contribute to outcomes, such as organizational structure, human resources, administrative budget, IT, and legislation.

### *The Assessment Process*

Repeated assessments with a gap of two to three years provide information on the extent to which a country's tax administration is improving. Over time, as more assessments are done, a picture emerges of relative performance across countries, regions, and income groups. This picture assists in understanding the strengths of different administrative responses and informs thinking at a global level about which are the more effective approaches to tax administration. A TADAT assessment report does not recommend specific reforms or comment on the potential impact of ongoing reforms in tax administration. Rather, it highlights administrative weaknesses and provides the basis for discussions about reform goals and implementation strategies.

The assessment of indicators follows the same approach as in the Public Expenditure and Financial Accountability diagnostic tool to allow comparability. Each of TADAT's 51 measurement dimensions is assessed separately. The overall score for an indicator is based on the assessment of its individual dimensions. These are scored on a four-point "ABCD" scale, with A denoting that performance meets or exceeds international norms and D indicating that performance is inadequate.

TADAT assessment is usually commissioned by international agencies like the regional development bank, International Monetary Fund, World Bank, or Inter-American Development Bank and is conducted by an assessment team comprising three to four trained assessors. The report is finalized after securing the country's feedback.

## Revenue Performance: Forecasting of Revenues and Tax Gap Analysis

Solid analytics have to be in place for governments to make informed decisions on tax reform. A tax reform strategy should prioritize good revenue forecasting, analysis of the potential of the tax system, impact of changes in tax policy, and analysis of tax expenditures. The importance of tax analysis and revenue forecasting for DRM as well as for proper budget management, particularly for the medium-term fiscal framework, cannot be overemphasized.

Revenue forecasting is also useful for tax gap analysis and typically has the following objectives:

- *Assessing the revenue impacts of policy changes.* This assessment includes changes in tax policies, nontax policies (trade policies, industrial policies, business or financial regulations), and structural changes.
- *Appraising the revenue impacts of economic changes or shocks.* This appraisal includes gross domestic product (GDP) growth, devaluation, inflation, trade patterns, the political situation in neighboring countries, and long drought, among others.
- *Measuring tax capacity and tax effort.* This assessment includes measuring the quantity and quality of revenue forecasts, the potential tax revenue of the economy, and the degree to which the revenue potential has been achieved.
- *Monitoring and measuring the performance of the revenue department.* This measurement provides a benchmark for monitoring collection performance and tax effort, which can be linked to bonus schemes.
- *Strengthening tax administration.* Such efforts include, for example, identifying improvements and expanding the tax base under existing tax legislation.
- *Determining the institutional setup.* Whether the tax policy unit (TPU) or the tax administration should prepare the forecast must be ascertained. Revenue forecasting is a central function of the ministry of finance, and the TPU has a crucial role to play. The tax administration should be responsible for collecting taxes, not for estimating revenue. The TPU should be responsible for estimating revenue, but cannot do so without data from the tax administration, which is in closer contact with taxpayers and is aware of the administrative factors affecting the collection of revenues.
- *Maintaining the database.* The quality of revenue forecasts is only as good as the quality of data. Data come from various sources, including the tax administration, statistical bureau, central bank, ministry of finance, and ministry of economy as well as trade or business organizations. The TPU should maintain and update the database on a continuous basis.
- *Coordinating closely with economic ministries, government agencies, and business organizations.* Coordination is essential to producing accurate economic forecasts. GDP is the source of all tax revenues, and accurate and timely GDP forecast is crucial. The department of statistics is a great source of supplementary data on income and expenditures, as it routinely conducts economic surveys. Chambers of commerce and industry also compile valuable data sets.

Four types of quantitative models are available for forecasting (Glenday, Shukla, and Sugana 2010):

- *Unconditional time-series analysis that includes trends and growth factor analysis.* This model is unconditional in the sense that forecasts are based only on past revenue data and use econometric techniques.
- *Macroeconomic or GDP-based modeling that uses time series of tax revenues and their bases.* This model relies on the link between growth of revenue and

growth of tax bases or GDP. The data requirement is limited to time series of tax revenues and time series of tax base—consumption, income, imports, or simply GDP.

- *Microsimulation models that are based on tax returns of individual taxpayers or transactions and then aggregate the results*. These models also enable estimation of the distributional effect on taxpayers of a given policy change. These models are data intensive and use microsimulation modeling techniques.
- *Revenue receipts modeling that monitors and projects short-term receipts by type of tax or aggregate revenues*. This modeling is especially useful for setting up monthly or quarterly targets for monitoring revenue collections. Data requirements are simple and limited to monthly receipts in the year of forecast along with monthly receipts in the previous 12 months.

All of these models can be used for all types of taxes—PIT, CIT, VAT, and excises. Microsimulation models are particularly useful for PIT and CIT. These models are in two parts. First, the typical taxpayer model analyzes the impact of a change in tax policy on a typical taxpayer and the aggregate forecast model analyzes the impact of a change in policy on aggregate revenue. The former is useful for studying the distributional impact of a tax policy change on taxpayers, while the latter is essential for estimating revenue. For VAT revenues, the input-output table model is most effective not only for forecasting revenue but also for accurately estimating the consumption base and the impact of exemptions and zero-rating. For trade taxes, harmonized codes up to between four and six digits are used to assess the impact of sectoral revision in tariff rates.

For forecasting royalties and CIT revenues from natural resources, production plans of mining and oil companies are helpful. However, this approach involves the forecasting of commodity prices, which can be difficult, and stochastic models, which may be necessary to model prices more precisely.

For forecasting revenue from property taxes, the property value base responds to real economic growth as demand for land and buildings increases and the revenue base expands, possibly with a lag of one to three years. Alternatively, property taxes can be forecast using microsimulation models with the help of a geographic information system database, global positioning system, and web-based computing.

For forecasting revenue from user fees, the base and rate are usually set by the local or regional governments. The forecasting exercise is thus reduced to forecasting the base, which mainly involves forecasting the population and number of users.

For estimating income from subnational income and sales taxes and excises, the same techniques are applied as for national taxes. Piggy-backing these assessments on national or state taxes makes it easier to estimate revenue.

Business license revenues are not so buoyant but are easy to forecast, as local government typically has data on the business licenses issued and sets the license fees. The GDP growth rate may be used as a proxy for business growth.

Once revenue is forecast to a fair degree of certainty, the forecast is compared with actual tax collections, yielding a measure of the tax gap. This analysis can be done by the type of tax.

A sound revenue-forecasting system has the following features:

- *Dedicated, full-time qualified staff.* Building revenue-forecasting expertise requires time and skill, particularly staff with proficiency in tax economics and econometrics. Capacity-building programs should be systematic and frequent.
- *Ability to anticipate data needs and construct suitable databases.* Policy makers may propose change in tax policy whose revenue impacts cannot be estimated accurately on the basis of only the existing data. Tax returns and household or industrial survey forms may have to be modified or redesigned, and staff in this unit should be able to do this.
- *Adequate hardware and software.* Staff should be well equipped with both state-of-the-art hardware as well as cutting-edge software.

## Human Resource Management Strategy

Tax administrations rely heavily on their personnel to carry out core functions, and the wage bill for staff often exceeds 80 percent of total operating costs. For this reason, human resource management is a key issue. Tax administrations invest heavily in their employees and need to have a human resources department that assists in management and supports the tax administration's fundamental need to use high-performing employees effectively. Improving HRM is a key strategy in reducing overhead costs, increasing quality, and raising more revenues (Osinski, Lethbridge, and Hinsz 2013).

### Responsibilities of the Human Resources Department

As part of the business planning process, the human resources department should work closely with line managers to identify the resources needed to execute strategic and operational business plans as well as to handle day-to-day administrative issues. Its activities include attracting, selecting, retaining, developing, motivating, and effectively using employees. The roles of the department and line managers extend to a wide range of functions, such as selection and placement, training and development, performance management, compensation, evaluation of staff, and accountability.

HRM is particularly critical in an environment where tax administrations are continuously moving toward greater automation. Most of the time a major transformation of the workforce is needed, which involves reducing the number of relatively low-skill positions and scaling up the number of high-skill positions in areas such as audit, investigation, taxpayer services, and so on. Prior to making decisions about increasing staff in specific areas, workload analysis and future projections are needed to reallocate personnel internally in the most efficient way. In addition, the tax administration should have a strategic human resource planning system to predict and meet its future employment requirements. This planning process takes into account workload projections and envisaged institutional changes and modernization programs.

### Main Components of HRM
The following are the main components of a modern and efficient HRM function:

- *Strategy.* Development of an HRM strategy, policies, and systems to support the tax administration's business strategy
- *Autonomy.* Empowerment of the revenue agency to make decisions about matters such as recruitment, retention, performance management, promotion, career planning, training and development, dismissal, and retirement
- *Policies and practices.* Human resource policies and practices that motivate, support, and protect employees
- *Training and development strategy.* A long-term training and development strategy for employees
- *Structure and systems.* An organizational structure and system to support the delivery of employee training and development needs.

In recent years, tax administrations have been reducing and reshaping their workforce to meet emerging needs and priorities. All revenue agencies today face an environment of changing risks, increasing work volume, growing complexity in laws and regulations, and rising community expectations. The technological advances are having a major impact both on tax administrations and on clients. All of these factors increase the need for an HRM strategy that will enable revenue agencies not only to meet their current needs but also to face future challenges.

### International Best Practices
The OECD has analyzed some aspects of HRM strategies and major policy changes implemented by revenue administrations around the world using surveys, annual reports, and other sources (OECD 2015). This study of both OECD and some non-OECD countries has identified key points and good practices for an effective HRM strategy that should serve as guidelines for LMICs that are reforming their tax administration.

#### Aspects of an HRM Strategy
The vast majority (88 percent) of revenue agencies have chalked out a formal HRM strategy based on an assessment of current and future skills and capability needs.

About two-thirds of tax administrations have planned major changes in their policies in one or more of the areas of recruitment, training, performance, or rewards. Many revenue bodies have plans for making significant changes to policies regarding training and development.

Most revenue agencies periodically survey staff on their levels of satisfaction, engagement, and motivation and share survey results with staff. Most (84 percent) also consult with staff when considering responses to survey findings.

### Staff Recruitment, Appointment, and Development

With a few exceptions, most revenue agencies have a fair degree of autonomy for managing staff recruitment, subject to budgetary limits set by the finance ministry; some revenue bodies are subject to government staff recruitment freezes.

Most revenue agencies (93 percent) are able to recruit staff and make appointments based on clearly defined qualification and experience criteria.

Most revenue bodies have staff development initiatives in place to increase commercial awareness and risk management capability (89 percent); around two-thirds (68 percent) of revenue bodies undertake such measures using external networks.

### Performance Management and Remuneration

Most revenue bodies (82 percent) have performance management systems in place, although about 20 percent do not set objectives for each member at the beginning of the performance period; the vast majority of revenue bodies (92 percent) review the performance of each staff member at least annually.

Most revenue bodies (80 percent) tie staff remuneration directly or broadly to public sector pay scales; the rest have unique arrangements. More than two-thirds have some flexibility to reward good performance.

### Overall Staffing Levels and Attrition

The majority of revenue bodies (60 percent) have experienced net reductions in staffing in the past five years, including Canada, Greece, the United Kingdom, and the United States.

Attrition rates vary considerably, ranging from 0.9 percent (Malaysia) to 13 percent (Mexico), but are generally at the lower end of this range.

### Capacity-Building Programs

Finally, a capacity-building strategy is needed to align staff skills more closely with business needs and to keep their skills updated. Although the government may have a training function responsible for delivering training courses applicable across government agencies, tax administrations need to develop specialized technical training for their own staff. Increasingly, revenue agencies are outsourcing training for management and leadership-related skills to universities and private companies. Due to the technical nature of their work and the scarcity of candidates with the necessary technical skills, tax administrations need to train staff. According to the OECD, 90 percent of tax administrations conduct assessments of their current and future skills and capability needs and develop a plan to fill any gaps.

Training at the induction stage is far from adequate. Training needs are bound to vary with the age and experience of staff as well as maturity of the revenue agency itself. Mid-career programs are needed to meet the evolving needs of both tax-related technical knowledge as well as soft skills like ethics, negotiations, teamwork, and leadership.

The Internal Revenue Service of Chile organizes educational courses with durations ranging from five weeks to five months. These courses are dedicated to teamwork, decision making, stress and time management, assertiveness, communication, and personal development.

India's Central Board of Direct Taxes has developed a capacity-building program for its revenue officers at different levels of their career, starting from 8–10 years of seniority and work experience to 16–18 years and finally 26–28 years. These six-week programs include four weeks in India and two weeks in a foreign university known for its expertise in taxation. Officers have to complete the program in their seniority group before they are considered for promotion to the next phase of their career.

## Notes

1. This chapter draws on several studies by the Organisation for Economic Co-operation and Development, U.S. Agency for International Development, the World Bank, and International Monetary Fund in the past decade, which are referenced throughout the text.

2. The U.S. tax administration was initially organized by type of tax, then by functions performed during the 1950s–90s, and then by type of taxpayer in 1998 (Internal Revenue Service Restructuring and Reform Act), with four main divisions: wage and investment income, small business and self-employed, large and mid-size business, and tax-exempt and government entities. Australia's and New Zealand's administrations originally were structured by type of tax, then changed to functional form, and finally were restructured by type of taxpayer or client in the early 1990s.

3. For discussion, see Jacobs (2013).

4. This section draws on Jimenez (2013).

5. In a survey of small and medium businesses in South Africa, Abrie and Doussy (2006) found that demand for an improved taxpayers' helpdesk was greater than demand for a simplified tax regime or a higher VAT threshold.

6. In a survey of Tanzanian taxpayers in late 1990s, 75 percent of respondents favored publishing the names of tax evaders and more than 80 percent favored publishing the names of persons receiving any kind of tax incentives or exemptions, along with the costs to the treasury (Gray 2001).

7. Hodges (2013) provides an excellent analysis of taxpayer services.

8. Research is being undertaken in Ireland and other countries in the European Union and the OECD to improve knowledge of the motives of taxpayers and their behavior toward taxation (Walsh 2012). Datta and Mullainathan (2012) discuss the design of this research.

9. Document published by the U.K. Cabinet Office, Behavioral Insights Team (2012).

# References

Abrie, W., and Elza Doussy. 2006. "Tax Compliance Obstacles Encountered by Small and Medium Enterprises in South Africa." *Meditari Accountancy Research* 14 (1): 1–13.

ADB (Asian Development Bank). 2014. *A Comparative Analysis of Tax Administration in Asia and the Pacific.* Manila: ADB.

Andreoni, James, Brian Erard, and Jonathan Feinstein. 1998. "Tax Compliance." *Journal of Economic Literature* 36 (2): 818–60.

Boame, Attah. 2009. "A Panel Analysis of Behavior Change in Individual Income Tax Compliance." In *Recent Research on Tax Administration and Compliance: Selected Papers Given at the 2008 IRS Research Conference.* IRS Research Bulletin 1500, Statistics of Income Division, Internal Revenue Service, Washington, DC.

Bobek, Donna, Robin Roberts, and John Sweeney. 2007. "The Social Norms of Tax Compliance: Evidence from Australia, Singapore, and the United States." *Journal of Business Ethics* 74 (1): 49–64.

Coleman, Stephen. 2007. "The Minnesota Income Tax Compliance Experiment: Replication of the Social Norms Experiment." MPRA Paper 5820, University Library of Munich, Germany. http://mpra.ub.uni-muenchen.de/5820/.

Datta, Saugato, and Sendhil Mullainathan. 2012. "Behavioral Design: A New Approach to Development Policy." CGD Policy Paper 016, Center for Global Development, Washington, DC. http://www.cgdev.org/content/publications/detail/1426679.

Fjeldstad, Odd-Helge, and Mick Moore. 2007. "Taxation and State-Building: Poor Countries in a Globalized World." CMI Working Paper WP 2007:11, Chr. Michelsen Institute, University of Bergen, Bergen.

Glenday, Graham, Gangadhar P. Shukla, and Rubino Sugana. 2010. "Revenue Forecasting: Issues and Techniques." Duke Center for International Development, Duke University, Durham, NC.

Gray, Clive. 2001. "Enhancing Transparency in Tax Administration in Madagascar and Tanzania." African Economic Policy Discussion Paper 77, U.S. Agency for International Development, Washington, DC.

Hodges, Yassie. 2013. "Taxpayer Services." In *Detailed Guidelines for Improved Tax Administration in Latin America and the Caribbean*, ch. 6. Paris: U.S. Agency for International Development.

Jacobs, Arturo. 2013. "Organizational Structure and Management." In *Detailed Guidelines for Improved Tax Administration in Latin America and the Caribbean*, ch. 4. Paris: U.S. Agency for International Development.

Jimenez, Guillermo. 2013. "Information Technology." In *Detailed Guidelines for Improved Tax Administration in Latin America and the Caribbean*, ch. 12. Paris: U.S. Agency for International Development.

KPMG Peat Marwick. 1995. "Government of Jamaica/World Bank—Tax Administration Reform Project—V.1: SOMC Broad Strategic Plan and Technical Report for Master Plan." KPMG Peat Marwick, Amstelveen, the Netherlands.

Lethbridge, Colin. 2013. "Audit." In *Detailed Guidelines for Improved Tax Administration in Latin America and the Caribbean*, ch. 8. Paris: U.S. Agency for International Development.

OECD (Organisation for Economic Co-operation and Development). 2010. "Understanding and Influencing Taxpayers' Compliance Behavior." Compliance Subgroup, Forum on Tax Administration, OECD, Paris.

———. 2011. "Tax Administration in OECD Countries: Comparative Information Series (2010)." Compliance Subgroup, Forum on Tax Administration, OECD, Paris.

———. 2015. *Tax Administration 2015: Comparative Information on OECD and Other Advanced and Emerging Economies*. Paris: OECD.

Osinski, Diana, Colin Lethbridge, and Suzanne Hinsz. 2013. "Human Resource Management and Organizational Development." In *Detailed Guidelines for Improved Tax Administration in Latin America and the Caribbean*, ch. 13. Washington, DC: U.S. Agency for International Development.

U.K. Cabinet Office, Behavioral Insights Team. 2012. *Applying Behavioral Insights to Reduce Fraud, Error, and Debt*. London: U.K. Cabinet Office.

Walsh, Keith. 2012. "Understanding Taxpayer Behavior: New Opportunities for Tax Administration." *Economic and Social Review* 43 (3): 451–75.

Wenzel, Michael. 2005. "Motivation or Rationalization? Causal Relations between Ethics, Norms, and Tax Compliance." *Journal of Economic Psychology* 26 (4): 491–508.

## CHAPTER 5

# World Bank's Role in Domestic Resource Mobilization

## Entry Points for the World Bank

The World Bank employs its expertise and resources to assist low- and middle-income countries (LMICs) in the reform of tax policy and tax administration. In particular, the current lending portfolio includes about 60 operations with tax components, ranging from business taxation policy to tax administration modernization. In addition, for years the Bank has delivered analytical work and technical assistance to client countries in the area of tax reform, including international taxation. In the current global context and given emerging issues, the emphasis on domestic resource mobilization (DRM), and commitment to the Addis Tax Initiative, how can the World Bank find new entry points, reinforce its commitment to tax reform, and enhance and expand its current tax agenda?

The Bank has vast experience in various fields that directly affect revenue mobilization, bringing decades of experience in supporting tax reform—both in policy and in administration—to mobilize domestic resources.

The Bank's work on public expenditure is an excellent entry point for policy dialogue on tax administration reforms with governments in most LMICs. The Bank has worked extensively in tax administration reforms at the request of host governments and executed projects in support of public expenditure management. The Bank's focus on public expenditure management gives it unique insight into revenue matters, as expenditure and revenue are two sides of the same coin. This focus enables the Bank to take a pragmatic view of revenue measures as part of the overall public financial management in a country.

Since the early 1990s, the Bank has worked on public expenditure and tax reforms largely through resident programs but also, in some cases, jointly with the International Monetary Fund or in collaboration with the Organisation for Economic Co-operation and Development. Based on the projects that closed in 1999–2014, the Bank had more than 250 loan operations in almost 100 countries with components dealing with some aspects of tax system reform—lending projects with at least 15 percent tax components and advisory services with at least 25 percent tax components (Subhash and Webb 2015).

There is a growing need to create links between taxation, accountability, expenditures, and broader state-building goals. The challenge for LMICs is to improve voluntary compliance among a large number of citizens and enterprises by establishing legitimacy of the tax system. With the breadth of its sectoral and subject matter expertise and its extensive work with governments on wider issues of governance, including taxation, development, and state building, the Bank has a distinct advantage in this area.

The Bank has broad experience in the area of tax policy and tax administration diagnostics, including issues such as tax incidence; tax gap analysis; tax expenditures; fiscal projections and microsimulation revenue forecasting; compliance analysis; productivity and efficiency measures in value added tax and corporate income tax; tobacco tax reforms; the Tax Administration Diagnostic Assessment Tool (TADAT) and the Integrated Assessment Model for Tax Administration (IAMTAX) mapping, risk assessment, and statistical tools; tax administration models and compliance management for various taxes; subnational taxes; transfer pricing diagnostics; treaty analysis; information technology; capacity building; and international taxation. The list goes on.

The Bank has developed information and communication technology (ICT) and human resource assessment tools that help to understand and assess the human and institutional capacity gaps of a tax administration. Modernization of a tax administration requires continuous advancement of technology as well as increasing automation of core business areas. Tax administrations have to process huge volumes of information in a timely and reliable way in order to reduce the costs of administration and compliance and increase the reliability, accuracy, and timeliness of the information processed. ICT development can also support the dissemination of taxpayer services and information online. The provision of tax services online will lead to significant changes in the organizational structure and business processes of tax administration.

Sophisticated computer applications alone are not enough to transform organizations. It is also important to address the human and institutional gaps that many LMICs face and to promote change management to overcome internal and external resistance to change. Strengthening the human resources framework is vital to overcoming challenges related to human capacity and institutional arrangements.

## DRM Strategy

A DRM strategy should provide a conceptual framework to address key shortcomings in the resource mobilization systems of LMICs. The strategy should seek to facilitate increased tax collection in order to provide countries with a stable and predictable fiscal environment and to promote growth, equity, and development. Achieving this objective requires implementing effective tax policy and administration conducive to putting in place tax systems that are broad, simple, and equitable and that facilitate taxpayer compliance. There is also a need to assess the adequacy of the Bank's lending and nonlending instruments for reform of tax and revenue administration.

## Pillars of the Proposed Strategy

The proposed strategy hinges on three pillars:

1. Enhancing the quality of tax systems (increasing tax collection but also minimizing economic distortions and reducing inequality)
2. Strengthening the operational capacity of tax administrations in terms of both administrative and policy aspects
3. Fostering social acceptance and legitimacy of the tax system, while improving public accountability (for example, reaching out to civil society).

Steps to take in this direction include simplifying taxes, strengthening tax administrations, and enhancing the role of subnational governments (table 5.1). Tax administration is part of the equation insofar as it guarantees fair implementation of the tax system and, as a result, ensures that everybody pays his or her fair share of tax revenue. Tax reforms should aim to strengthen governance,

**Table 5.1 Key Elements of a DRM Strategy (Governance-Focused Reform Agenda)**

| Key principles | Objectives | Building blocks |
|---|---|---|
| Centrality of DRM in development | • Place DRM at the center of development.<br>• Develop a strong analytical framework to help countries to establish productive, efficient, and equitable tax systems at both the national and the subnational levels and to tailor World Bank advice to the specific context of the region. | 1. Tax policy<br>2. Revenue administration (tax administration and customs)<br>3. Taxpayer service, public awareness, transparency, and civil society engagement<br>4. Information and communication technologies (information technology systems aligned with core processes of tax administration)<br>5. Political economy of tax policy and revenue administration reform<br>6. Subnational taxation<br>7. Legal functions (tax appeals and relations with courts and tribunals)<br>8. Cross-cutting issues (knowledge management and human resources) |
| Innovation and flexibility | • Focus on the context and emphasize innovation and flexibility.<br>• Achieve sufficiency in terms of revenue collection as measured by a reduction in the tax compliance gap. | |
| State building through accountability and transparency | • Recognize taxation as a key driver for state building and accountability and tax reform as a possible contributor to broader gains in state capacity and quality of governance.<br>• Enhance the capacities and capabilities of the tax administration. | |
| Primacy of politics in tax reform | • Adopt an increasingly political approach to tax reform, as tax reform is profoundly political and demands careful understanding of political barriers and opportunities.<br>• Put in place tools to assist countries in measuring performance of their revenue administration. | |
| Broader context of public sector reform | • Generate revenues only when additional funds translate into high-quality social expenditure.<br>• Build a multidisciplinary team specializing in tax policy and tax administration. | |

*table continues next page*

**Table 5.1  Key Elements of a DRM Strategy (Governance-Focused Reform Agenda)** *(continued)*

| Key principles | Objectives | Building blocks |
|---|---|---|
| Results-oriented approach | • Take a results-oriented approach to public sector reform, including the revenue and expenditure sides of public finance and the impact of public sector reform on improved public service delivery; look at both revenue and expenditure sides of the equation.<br>• Coordinate the World Bank's analytical work on public expenditures with the work on domestic revenue mobilization in low- and middle-income countries.<br>• Focus on results and devise flexible instruments such as combining lending with technical assistance to provide flexibility. | |
| Performance | • Measure performance of revenue administration to monitor World Bank project results and understand whether the revenue administration is doing a good job or at least the best job possible under the circumstances.<br>• Develop models and indicators to measure performance of tax administration and customs beyond revenue collections alone. | |
| Coordination | • Coordinate with other international financial institutions, donors, regional organizations, and other actors involved in providing technical assistance on tax matters.<br>• Coordinate with other Global Practices working in the tax area in the World Bank. | |

*Note:* DRM = domestic resource mobilization.

improve the business environment, and support formalization of the economy. These reforms should also extend to subnational and local governments and seek to generate more revenue at these levels.

### Building Blocks of Bank Engagement

The strategic framework encompasses the entire cycle of the tax process, ranging from a taxpayer registry to tax appeals and judicial cases. Eight building blocks are envisioned that will provide a strategic umbrella for potential World Bank engagement.

#### Tax Policy

Tax policy includes tax simplification, tax and inequality, tax incentives, international dimension of taxation, transfer pricing, tax transparency, small and medium enterprise taxation, behavioral economics analysis of tax systems, and estimation of the tax gap.

#### Revenue Policy

Revenue administration encompasses tax administration and customs. A well-designed tax policy can be undermined by a poorly administered tax. It also works the other way around, and enhancing the operational capacity of tax administration effectively and efficiently is instrumental to promoting fairness in application of the tax system. The following are possible areas of work:

- For the revenue authority, the merger or division of customs and tax administration, core processes of tax administration, taxpayer registration, tax audit, and tax arrears
- For the institutional structure, the outsourcing of tax administration processes, organizational structure, nontax functions, and anticorruption strategies
- For the exchange of information, the administration of tax systems without borders and operational processes of a customs administration.

### Compliance
Enhancing public awareness, transparency, and civil society engagement are crucial to increasing voluntary compliance and achieving the higher goals of state building and broader public sector reforms. Compliance can be increased with better government standards, because taxpayers then have greater confidence that their taxes will be well spent.

### ICTs
Information and communication technologies are useful for aligning systems with core processes of tax administration. They facilitate data collection, preserve integrity of data, and expedite the overall tax administration process.

### Political Economy
Assessments and technical assistance that are restricted to technical, apolitical aspects of tax reform have failed to capture the reality of tax policy making in many countries. This failure is rooted in the fact that tax reform affects the distribution of resources and almost invariably confronts strong vested interests opposed to reform. If there is committed leadership, both within and outside of the ministry of finance and tax administration, tax reform is more likely to succeed. It is important for reform efforts to be informed by an understanding of political opportunities and constraints, which may guide the content of reform efforts, their priority, their timing, and the strategies adopted.

### Subnational Taxation
What is own-source subnational revenue? Who levies which revenues (revenue assignment)? Are there vertical and horizontal imbalances? What are the options for administering subnational revenues, property taxation, and vehicle taxes?

### Tax Appeals and Judicial Tax Cases
Statistical analysis is needed of tax appeals and judicial disputes, as is coordination between tax administration and courts. Enhanced dispute resolution services for taxpayers can increase the overall confidence in the tax administration and, in turn, improve compliance.

### Cross-Cutting Issues

Two cross-cutting issues are knowledge management and human resources. A knowledge management strategy needs to be delineated in order to provide Bank staff with specialized knowledge of tax issues and to align Bank products better with modern trends in tax policy and revenue administration. A knowledge management dissemination strategy is also required.

In human resources, the complexities involved in administering tax systems require trained and skilled staff, especially in core business areas such as tax audit or tax arrears management. Topics covered by a human resources management system include recruitment, staff development, staff satisfaction, remunerations and benefits, leadership and talent management, and staff turnover, among others. In addition, the tax administration should have a strategic human resource planning system to predict and meet its future employment requirements. This planning process takes into account workload projections and envisaged institutional changes and modernization programs.

### Focus on Results

A strong focus on results might shift demand away from input-based and toward results-based instruments and the increasing use of risk-advisory services instruments (table 5.2). A second position paper deals with results-based instruments and will be merged with this DRM report, specifically with the results of an impact analysis.

**Table 5.2  Measuring Results of Public Sector Reform**

| Public sector institution | Type of results | Measurement |
|---|---|---|
| Upstream bodies at the center of government | • Services, such as health or education, that are provided directly<br>• Management of infrastructure and other public investments<br>• Regulation of social and economic behavior, when necessary, such as food or road transport safety | • It is difficult to determine the strength of the causal relationship between the output and achievement of the policy objective.<br>• Causality in achieving public policy outcomes is hard to assign, making quality of outputs very hard to determine.<br>• Budgeting needs to emphasize performance, and a balanced score card system could be introduced in service agencies. |
| Downstream delivery bodies | • Outcomes that are the product of their own capacity (ensuring that public revenues, expenditures, and debt remain within agreed fiscal aggregates or maximizing cooperation between levels of government)<br>• Administrative procedures (design and enforcement of the rules of the game) that the downstream agencies must play by, for example, allocation and management of public finances, creation and management of employment regimes | • The World Bank has developed models to measure public sector performance, including tax administration, which provides a comprehensive analysis from different perspectives, namely, legal framework, institutional setup, and core functions or operations. |

*Source:* Manning 2014.

## Summary

A strategic approach to DRM is necessary as effective tax reform requires political will to overcome vested interests that benefit from existing arrangements. Reform is more likely to be more successful if pursued systematically across all areas, rather than in a piecemeal approach. Any improvement in tax administration, however significant, can be undermined by other parts of the process. New legislation that meets good international practices will not increase DRM if the tax system's operations are not concurrently improved to implement the new rules. Experience demonstrates that the window of opportunity to implement tax reforms is likely to be relatively short (for example, 12–24 months), as opposition to change often emerges. For example, the Tax Administration Reform Project in Pakistan encountered strong internal resistance from the tax authorities and required a new, more holistic approach. These issues imply that technical assistance and financing must be both strategic and rapidly deployable.

## References

Manning, Nick. 2014. "PSM Approach (2010–2012): How Can We Measure State Capacity?" World Bank, Washington, DC.

Subhash, Nepali, and Steven B. Webb. 2015. "Tax Project Data Analysis." World Bank, Washington, DC, December.

# APPENDIX A

# Revenue Trend Analysis

## Total Revenue

Total revenue in low-income countries (LICs) increased from 18 percent of gross domestic product (GDP) in 1990 to 21 percent in 2013, when revenue growth in countries at other income levels was relatively flat (figures A.1 and A.2). The steady, solid performance of the value added tax contributed to much of the growth in total revenue in LICs (figures A.3 and A.4). Revenue in upper-middle-income countries and in high-income countries was flat in this period due to a fall in revenue from trade transaction taxes (figures A.5 and A.6). Revenue from grants declined in lower-middle-income countries, balancing the rise in tax revenue and leading to flat total revenue collection during this period (figures A.7 and A.8).

**Figure A.1  Total Revenue as a Percentage of GDP, by Country Income Group, 1990–2013**

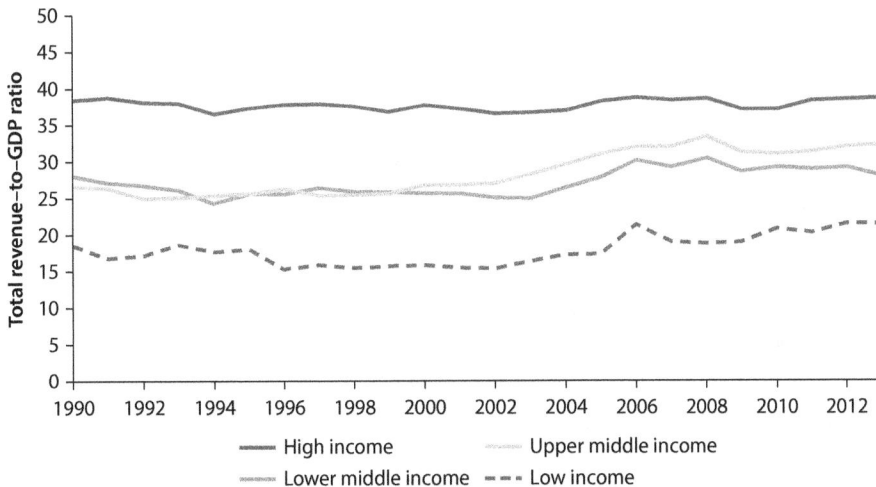

Source: International Monetary Fund, Fiscal Affairs Department database.
Note: GDP = gross domestic product.

**Figure A.2  Total Revenue as a Percentage of GDP, by Region, 1990–2012**

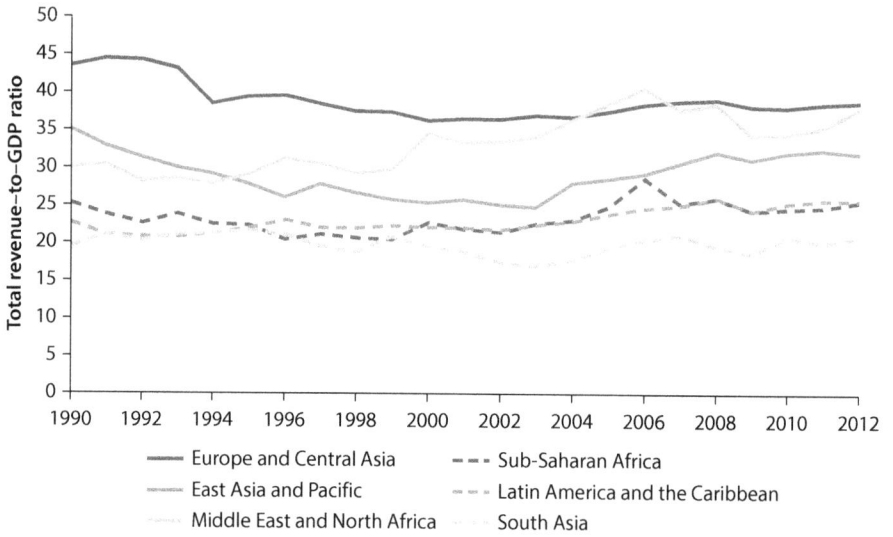

*Source:* International Monetary Fund, Fiscal Affairs Department database.
*Note:* GDP = gross domestic product.

**Figure A.3  Value Added Tax as a Percentage of GDP, by Country Income Group, 2000–12**

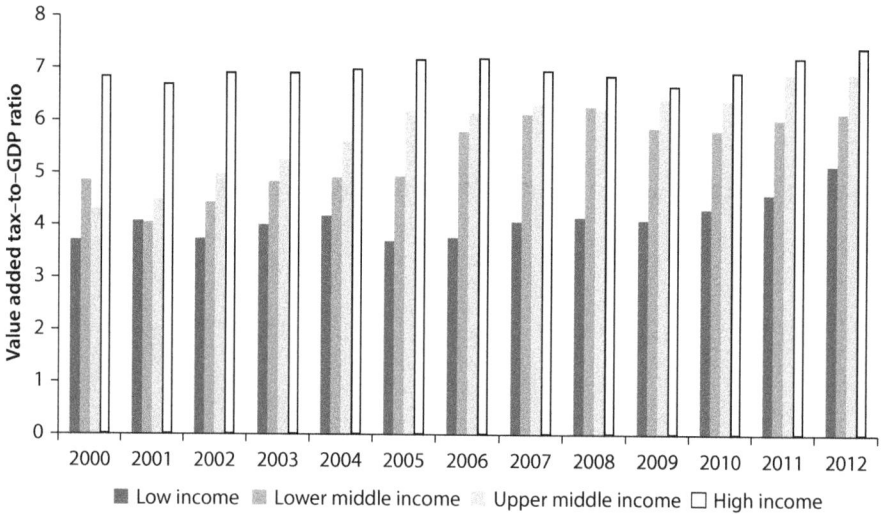

*Source:* International Monetary Fund, Fiscal Affairs Department database.
*Note:* GDP = gross domestic product.

**Figure A.4  Value Added Tax as a Percentage of GDP, by Region, 2000–12**

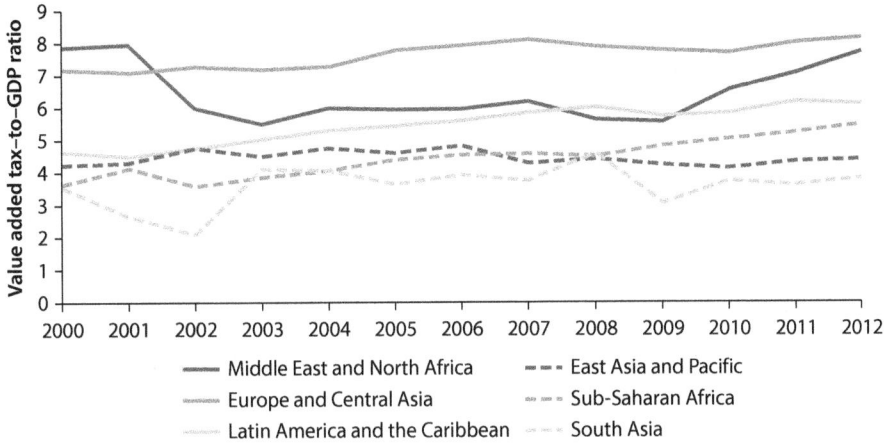

Source: International Monetary Fund, Fiscal Affairs Department database.
Note: GDP = gross domestic product.

**Figure A.5  Trade Transaction Tax as a Percentage of GDP, by Country Income Group, 2000–12**

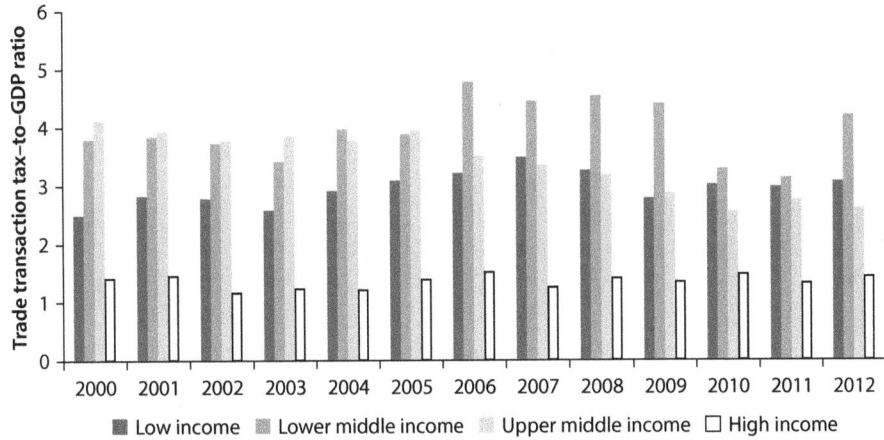

Source: International Monetary Fund, Fiscal Affairs Department database.
Note: GDP = gross domestic product.

**Figure A.6  Trade Transaction Tax as a Percentage of GDP, by Region, 2000–12**

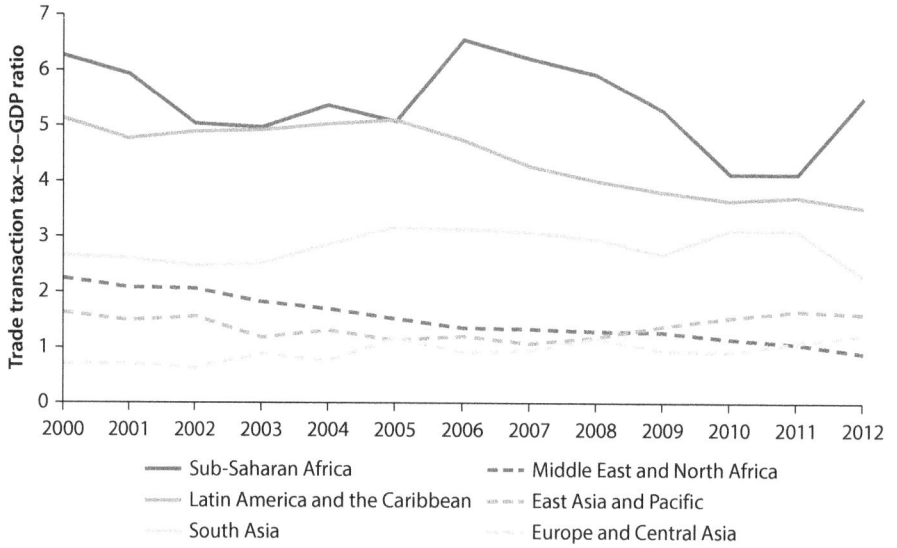

Legend:
- Sub-Saharan Africa
- Middle East and North Africa
- Latin America and the Caribbean
- East Asia and Pacific
- South Asia
- Europe and Central Asia

*Source:* International Monetary Fund, Fiscal Affairs Department database.
*Note:* GDP = gross domestic product.

**Figure A.7  Grants as a Percentage of GDP, by Country Income Group, 2000–12**

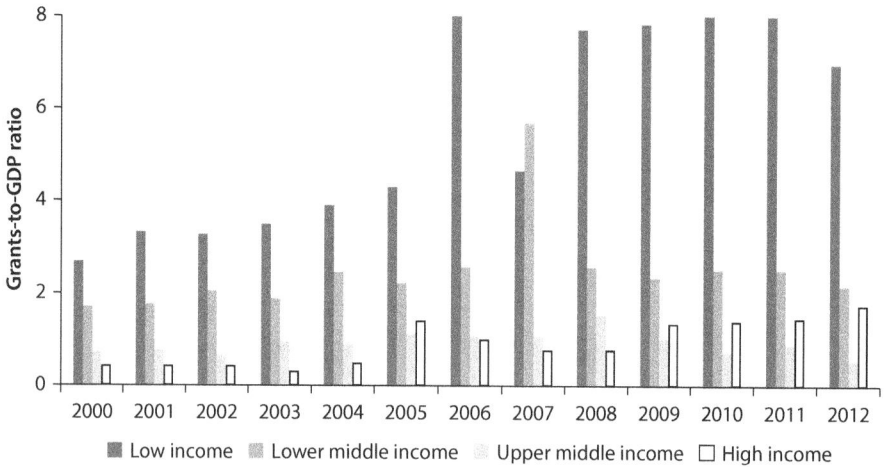

Legend: ■ Low income   ▨ Lower middle income   Upper middle income   ☐ High income

*Source:* International Monetary Fund, Fiscal Affairs Department database.
*Note:* GDP = gross domestic product

**Figure A.8  Grants as a Percentage of GDP, by Region, 2000–12**

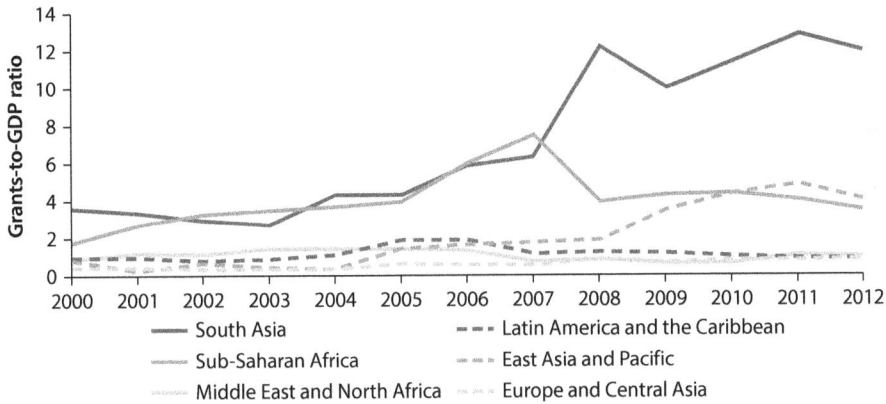

*Source:* International Monetary Fund, Fiscal Affairs Department database.
*Note:* GDP = gross domestic product.

## Tax Revenue

Total tax revenue rose from 11 percent to 14 percent of GDP in LICs and from 13 percent to 19 percent of GDP in lower-middle-income countries between 1990 and 2012 (figures A.9 and A.10).

### Trade Transaction Tax

The trade transaction tax constituted 28 percent of GDP in Lesotho between 2000 and 2012, but only 16 percent in 2010 and 18 percent in 2011. The decline in Lesotho could explain why trade transaction tax revenue dipped in Sub-Saharan Africa in 2010 and 2011 (figure A.6).

### Excises

Algeria's excise revenue constituted 9, 21, and 12 percent of GDP, respectively, in 2006, 2007, and 2008. This performance may explain the jump in excise revenue in the Middle East and North Africa in these years (figures A.11 and A.12).

### Property Tax

Mongolia's property tax constituted 7 percent of GDP in 2007, compared with only 0.9 percent between 2000 and 2012. This result caused a jump in property tax revenue in East Asia and the Pacific in 2007 (figures A.13 and A.14).

### Income Tax

Income taxes include taxes on income, profits, and capital gains generally levied on (a) compensation for labor services; (b) interest, dividends, rent, and royalty income; (c) capital gains and losses; (d) profits of corporations and partnerships; (e) taxable portions of social security, retirement account distributions, and life insurance; and (f) miscellaneous other income items (figures A.15–A.16).

**Figure A.9 Tax Revenue (Excluding Social Contributions) as a Percentage of GDP, by Country Income Group, 1990–2012**

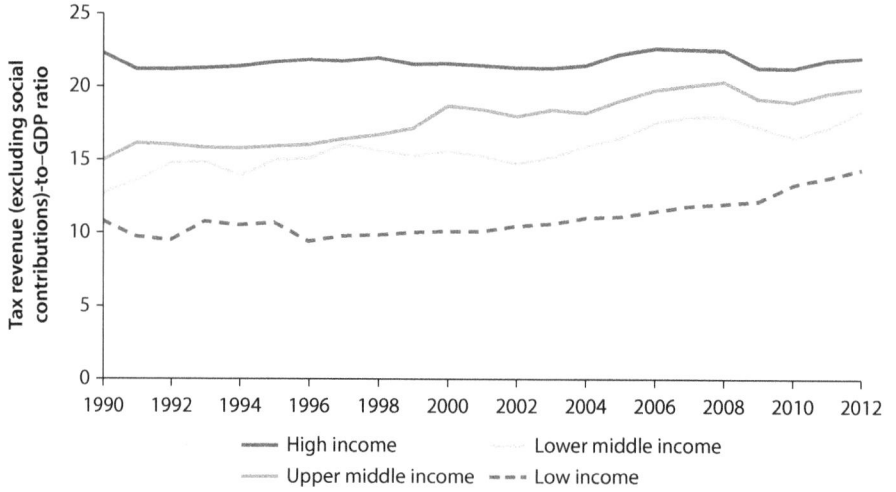

*Source:* International Monetary Fund, Fiscal Affairs Department database.
*Note:* GDP = gross domestic product.

**Figure A.10 Tax Revenue (Excluding Social Contributions) as a Percentage of GDP, by Region, 1990–2012**

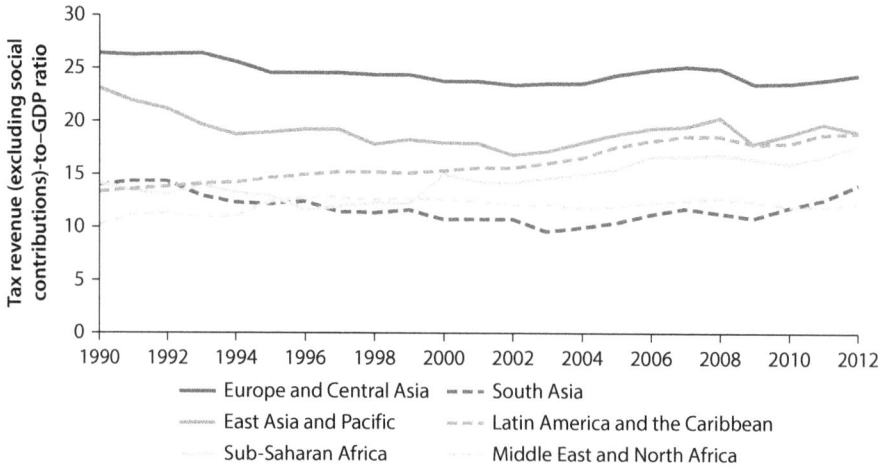

*Source:* International Monetary Fund, Fiscal Affairs Department database.
*Note:* GDP = gross domestic product.

**Figure A.11  Excises as a Percentage of GDP, by Country Income Group, 2000–12**

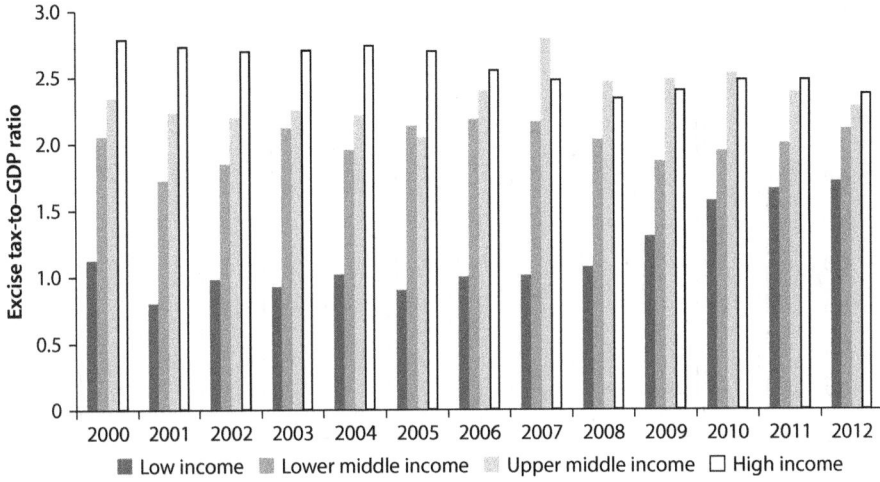

*Source:* International Monetary Fund, Fiscal Affairs Department database.
*Note:* GDP = gross domestic product.

**Figure A.12  Excises as a Percentage of GDP, by Region, 2000–12**

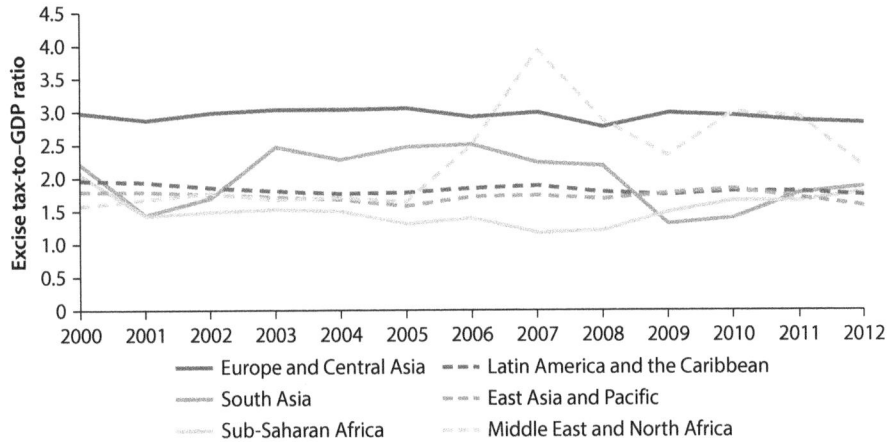

*Source:* International Monetary Fund, Fiscal Affairs Department database.
*Note:* GDP = gross domestic product.

**Figure A.13  Property Tax as a Percentage of GDP, by Country Income Group, 2000–12**

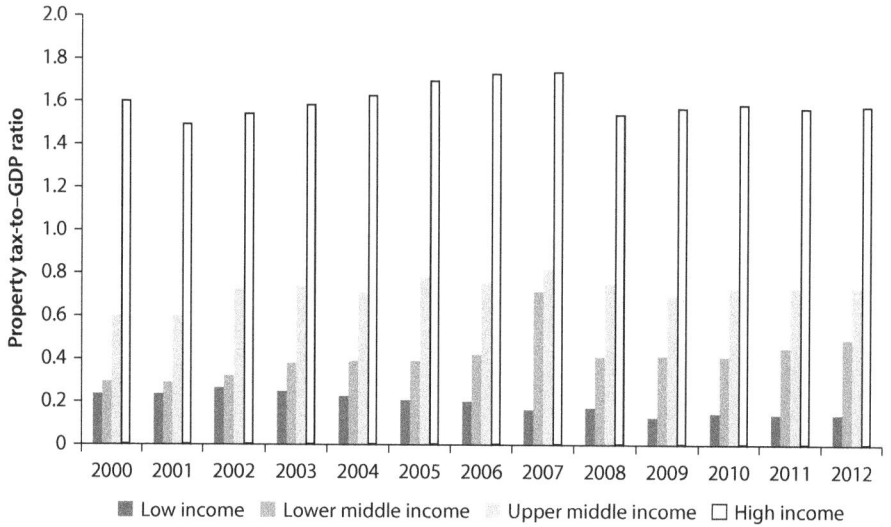

Source: International Monetary Fund, Fiscal Affairs Department database.
Note: GDP = gross domestic product.

**Figure A.14  Property Tax as a Percentage of GDP, by Region, 2000–12**

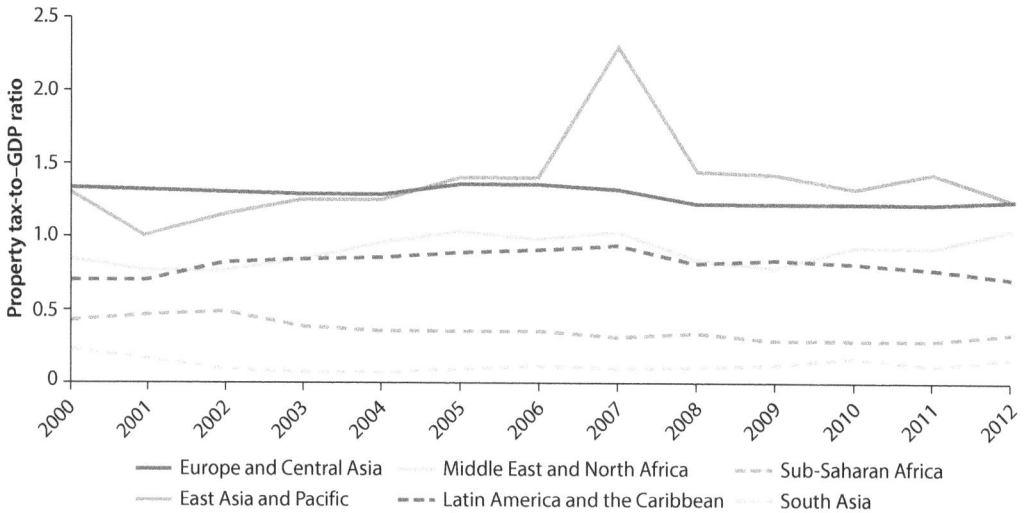

Source: International Monetary Fund, Fiscal Affairs Department database.
Note: GDP = gross domestic product.

**Figure A.15  Income Tax as a Percentage of GDP, by Country Income Group, 2000–12**

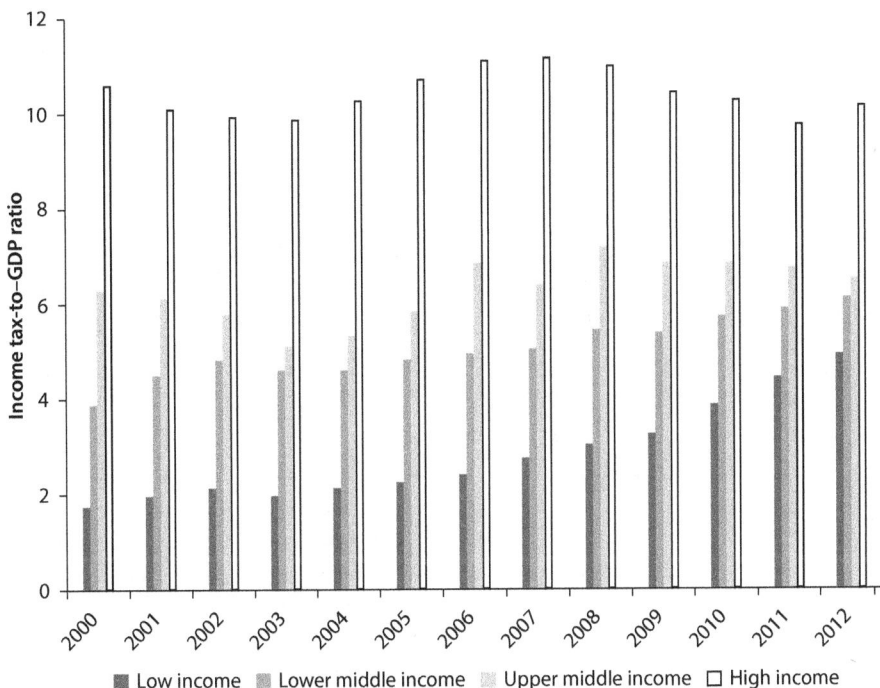

*Source:* International Monetary Fund, Fiscal Affairs Department database.
*Note:* GDP = gross domestic product.

**Figure A.16  Income Tax as a Percentage of GDP, by Region, 2000–12**

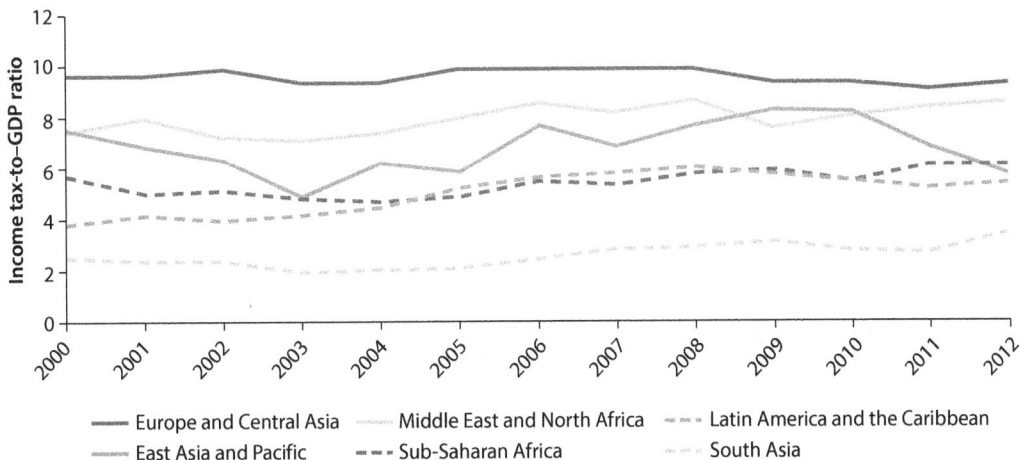

*Source:* International Monetary Fund, Fiscal Affairs Department database.
*Note:* GDP = gross domestic product.

**Figure A.17  Corporate Income Tax as a Percentage of GDP, by Income Group, 2000–12**

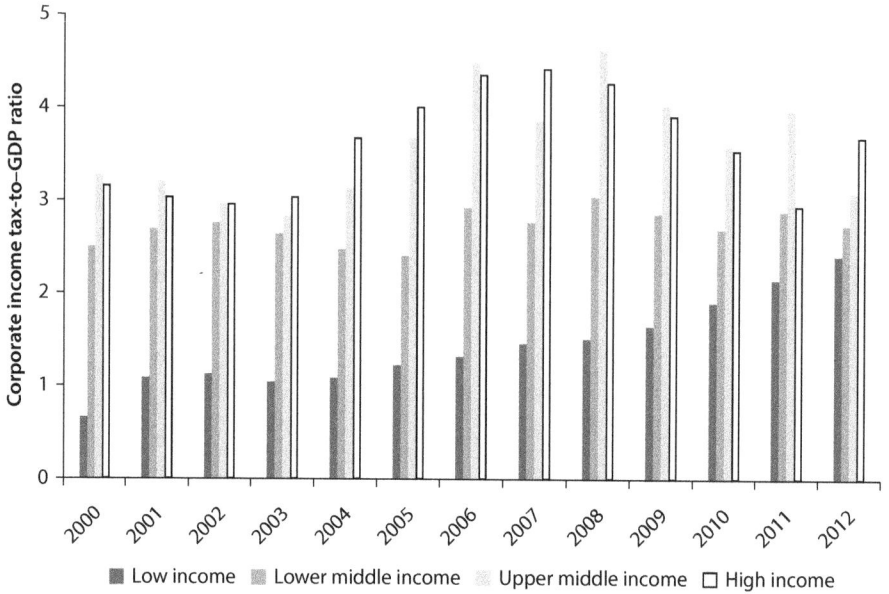

Source: International Monetary Fund, Fiscal Affairs Department database.
Note: GDP = gross domestic product.

**Figure A.18  Corporate Income Tax as a Percentage of GDP, by Region, 2000–12**

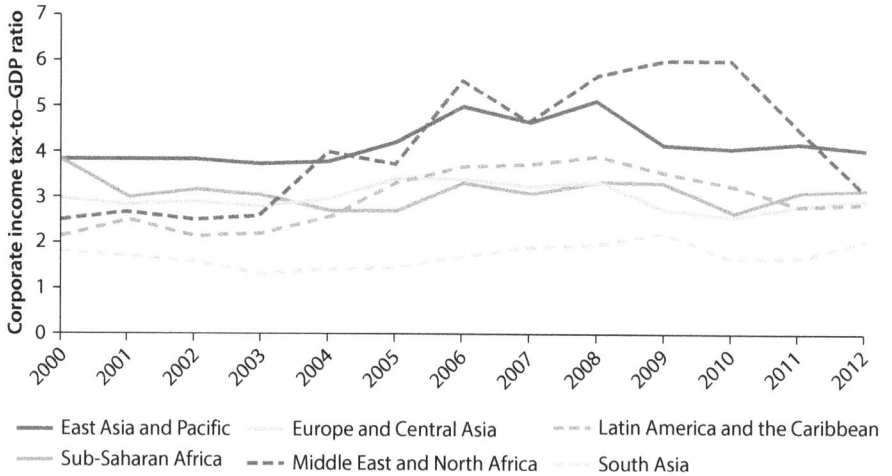

Source: International Monetary Fund, Fiscal Affairs Department database.
Note: GDP = gross domestic product.

The corporate income tax worldwide constituted 18.5 percent of GDP, on average, between 2004 and 2010, compared with only around 5 percent of GDP in the Middle East and North Africa (figures A.17 and A.18). Algeria had comparatively high corporate income tax collection in 2006 and the following years until 2011. This variability caused a jump in revenue from the corporate income tax in the Middle East and North Africa during the period between 2004 and 2010.

# Benchmark for Assessing Tax Systems

## A "Good" Tax System

The new generation of tax reforms should not focus exclusively on generating adequate government revenue; rather, it should also seek to create a system that improves the progressivity and distributional impact of taxes, creates minimum inefficiency, has a low cost of administration and compliance, contributes to business development and an investment-friendly environment, and ultimately promotes economic growth. Based on the theory and experience of the past several decades, the following principles of a "good" tax system are useful to keep in mind when assessing potential tax reforms.

### Equity

For reasons of social or political justice, tax systems should be "fair" or "equitable," with both *horizontal* and *vertical* equity. Horizontal equity implies that people in equal circumstances should be taxed equally—that is, they should pay the same percentage of their income in taxes. This requires a broad tax base so that some people are not left out of the tax net, while others manage to escape because their source of income is hard to tax. Much of the detail and complexity of tax law is due to the need to define a comprehensive tax base and deal with exceptional circumstances and cases.

Vertical equity implies that persons with greater ability to pay should pay a higher percentage of their income in taxes. This leads to progressive income taxes, where higher-income persons pay a higher share of their income in tax.

Equity in taxation is not only an esoteric notion; it also has direct bearing on domestic resource mobilization. A tax system that is not perceived to be fair and equitable does not elicit natural compliance from taxpayers and is hard to administer.

### Economic Efficiency

The transfer of resources to the public sector—the tax burden—usually involves an added cost to the economy that arises from distortions in the price system.

Taxes not only reduce the size of the private sector, but also change the prices (wage rates, interest rates, goods prices) in the economy. This distribution results in changes in the patterns of consumption, savings, work effort, investment, and international trade from the patterns that would have prevailed in the absence of taxes. These changes in the allocation of economic resources impose an excess burden or an efficiency cost. The tax structure should be designed to collect a given tax revenue with a minimum excess burden or economic efficiency cost.

High economic efficiency costs are generally related to high tax rates and to large differentials in tax rates among sectors, especially between the tax rates on close substitutes. The efficiency costs of consumption taxes also rise as price elasticities become higher—that is, there are good substitutes and either demand or supply is sensitive to price changes. Where price elasticities are very low (inelastic) for a group of similar goods, it may be justifiable to tax such goods at an above-average tax rate through the use of excises or special consumption taxes, typically on tobacco products and alcoholic beverages (sometimes labeled "sin" goods) and petroleum oil products. High income taxes distort the supply of productive factors to the marketplace, discourage the supply of labor, and distort the savings and investment decisions in the economy.

### Enhancing Efficiency through "Sin" Taxes and Green Tax Reform

This category of taxes improves rather than distorts economic efficiency. In the case of goods like tobacco products and alcoholic drinks and goods that pollute the environment such as motor fuels, fertilizers, and plastic bags, the private sector does not take into account the external costs imposed on the economy and consequently overproduces such goods. Consumption taxes in these cases restore the market equilibrium to its optimal level. In the absence of any tax on these products, the market ignores the negative externality. These taxes therefore enhance economic efficiency. The challenge is to assess the extent of distortion that the negative externality creates and to determine the right level of tax. The demand for many of these goods is less elastic—for example, for cigarettes, alcoholic drinks, and fuel to some extent—and taxes on these goods can generate a fair amount of revenue.

### Technical Efficiency

The administrative or transaction costs on the public sector and compliance costs on the private sector of transferring resources should be minimized so that maximum resources are available for public sector expenditures. This can be achieved by simplifying the tax structure and the administrative procedures, typically by making tax rates more uniform, withholding tax at source, and imposing simple, reasonable penalties and interest charges to induce compliance. Another approach is to remove nuisance taxes, where the administrative and compliance costs exceed revenues.

However, while excessive public spending on tax administration can be wasteful, spending too little can also be economically wasteful for at least two reasons. First, broad coverage of the tax base requires sufficient enforcement capacity.

Second, added administrative spending on taxpayer education and services can lower the transaction costs of complying with the tax and help to mobilize revenue. An increase in spending on taxpayer services and education may be more than offset by a reduction in the compliance costs of taxpayers, generally resulting in higher tax revenues.

While simplicity of tax laws usually reduces the costs of both administration and compliance, it also reduces coverage and equity. So tax systems should be simplified on the basis of due analysis.

### Stability of Tax Revenues

The overall tax revenue structure of an economy should generate adequate and stable revenue flows so that fiscal deficits and expenditure levels are predictable. Large fluctuations in revenue result in either unforeseen and costly debt financing or lower spending, particularly for development and capital investments and for service provision. An unexpected drop in revenue is often absorbed by some combination of inflationary financing—"crowding out" private investment through higher domestic borrowing, resorting to foreign debt obligations, and reducing expenditures by delaying development expenditures or reducing operating and maintenance expenditures—that ultimately lowers economic growth as well as the quality of public services. It is generally difficult to change tax laws or to upgrade tax effort quickly in response to an unexpected drop in revenue.

Revenue often fluctuates where the tax base is narrow, such as reliance on oil or mining revenues, which can fluctuate with world prices and demand. To ensure stable revenue, the tax structure should be revenue-elastic—revenue should grow at least as fast as gross domestic product (GDP), and the tax base should be *well diversified* to withstand shocks to the economy, such as fluctuations in world commodity prices. Revenue diversification is hard to achieve in small economies that depend on particular sectors or revenue sources. The key factors contributing to revenue stability are having a revenue base that grows with the economy and tax rates that tax at least a constant share of the growing base (ad valorem rates). If GDP is growing due to increased tourism or a growing services sector, tax revenue from traditional sectors such as manufacturing will not provide stable revenue.

### Tax Neutrality

Tax neutrality refers to a tax policy environment where economic decisions either are not affected or are minimally affected by tax factors. It implies achieving a "level playing field," where the tax system does not favor one group of taxpayers over another. Neutrality has different implications depending on the context. Basically, it means minimum intervention in the economy through the tax and other regulatory instruments.

The various principles of a "good" tax system are not always complementary; they are often in conflict, and trade-offs have to be made. For instance, equity and efficiency measures do not necessarily go together. Efficiency demands a lower and less differentiated tax structure, while equity demands lower tax rates on the income of poor people and on the goods and services consumed by them. Broadening the tax base generally improves horizontal equity, stability, and allocative efficiency of a tax. However, at some point, increase in the breadth of a tax base raises administrative costs through complicated laws, which cause higher transaction costs. Similarly, at times the revenue potential of a tax conflicts with the equity principle. A single-rate broad-based value added tax (VAT) may be administratively desirable and generate high VAT revenue but is generally regressive and imposes a higher tax burden on the low-income population. To meet the equity goals, it may be better to raise revenues using a regressive VAT and then to promote equity via the expenditure route through the budget.

Therefore, when it comes to policy design, policy makers have to make trade-offs with various, and in many cases competing, objectives regarding what they want tax reform to achieve. Both the complementarity and the trade-off effects have to be considered to achieve the requisite balance in a "good" tax system.

## Assessing Major Tax Regimes

If a country is to achieve adequate and stable revenue resources, it is important to examine critically the nature of existing taxes and the way they are being administered, keeping in view the criteria for a "good" tax system: efficiency, equity, revenue stability, technical efficiency, and neutrality. Assessing taxation policies within the broader challenges faced by a specific country must be demand driven. It also is supply driven to some extent, since the aid agency, which is armed with the knowledge and experience of international best practices, can inform and educate the country stakeholders appropriately and then arrive at an agreed plan of action.

Thus, there has to be a country-by-country diagnosis and strategy for tax reform. The following paragraphs present the criteria for each kind of tax to serve as guiding norms when assessing the tax system in low- and middle-income countries (LMICs).

### Tax Policy Unit in Ministry of Finance

For effective and efficient revenue mobilization, informed and careful analysis of policies and practices is essential. The starting point in assessing the tax system of a country should be to look at the role of the tax policy unit (TPU) in the ministry of finance. The TPU is where taxation, including incidence on taxpayers, is and should be analyzed. The first question in assessing the tax system in an LMIC is whether the TPU is functional; whether its duties and responsibilities are well defined; and whether it has the necessary resources, including skilled staff and authority, to perform its functions. The TPU should perform the following broad functions:

- *Monitor revenue potential and tax collections*. This includes estimating tax capacity and identifying tax handles with growth potential, analyzing the mix of tax and nontax revenue instruments, exploring the scope for charging user fees for public services wherever feasible, and establishing a reliable database and information system.

- *Evaluate economic and structural aspects of fiscal policy.* This includes analyzing the impact of consumption taxes on efficiency, incidence, and equity, exploring options for the design of income tax, using a microsimulation model, assessing the impact of changes in one tax regime on revenue from other taxes, and scrutinizing sources of nontax revenue and "nuisance taxes."
- *Analyze tax expenditures.* This includes quantifying the revenue impacts of (a) exemptions, (b) incentives, (c) credits, (d) rate relief, (e) subsidies, (f) tax deferrals, and (g) tariff exemptions for selected items, industries, and free zones in order to include tax expenditure in the budget for the sake of public debate and transparency.
- *Evaluate the impact of nontax economic policies.* Many economic policies not related directly to taxation have profound impacts on tax revenues. These include estimating the impacts of alternative premises about the economy, such as the economic growth rate or growth rate of specific economic sectors, and measuring the effect of changes in macroeconomic policy on the tax regime and tax revenues, such as (a) the removal of quantitative restrictions on imports, (b) trade liberalization policies and their effect on import substitution and export promotion, (c) deregulation of certain economic activities, (d) currency fluctuation, and (e) outcome of interest rate changes for business profits.
- *Forecast future tax revenues.* Forecasting is a central task of the unit and involves computing elasticity of various taxes and the entire tax system, evaluating the effect of inflation and price changes on tax revenues, and forecasting revenues from each type of tax.
- *Conduct tax gap analysis.* The tax gap is the gap between potential and actual tax revenue. This analysis examines the level of tax effort and compliance (revenue leakage). Since the TPU performs these tasks, it is well placed to assess the tax gap by each type of tax.

Addressing any shortcomings in the structure of the TPU should be the first step in tax policy reform.

### Value Added Tax

Modern VAT is generally based on consumption, follows the destination principle, uses the credit invoice method, and has either a single rate or multiple rates:

- The rate should be broad based and ideally only on exports that are zero rated, with minimum exemptions for equity or administrative considerations.
- The rate should be moderate to encourage compliance and generate adequate revenue, as very high rates may lead to evasion.
- Expenditures on pro-poor programs through the budget process are a better route for achieving equity than tampering with the tax base or the tax rate.

- The VAT should preferably be either a single or zero rate, as multiple rates may not promote equity and may complicate administration and compliance.
- Traders below a threshold should be exempt from the VAT for administrative expediency and, unless they are very small, be subject to a turnover tax.
- A threshold should be chosen considering the trade-off between cost of administration and revenue forgone.
- A reasonable refund system is essential for integrity of the VAT system.

### Excises or Special Consumption Tax

Excises are used mainly to generate revenue and discourage consumption of socially undesirable ("sin") goods. They are easy to administer because they are applied on a few select producers:

- The base should be narrow because excises are applied on only a few products and should ensure that all close substitutes are also in the tax net to avoid erosion of the tax base.
- They are generally levied at a single rate, either as a tax per unit or as an ad valorem tax.
- Unit taxes are best used to target some negative externality, for example, the amount of nicotine in cigarettes, alcoholic content in drinks, or pollutants in gasoline, but they need to be indexed to inflation and revised periodically because revenue otherwise falls over time; indexation is politically difficult to do on a regular basis.
- Ad valorem taxes are more revenue elastic.
- Excises should be applied in combination with value added taxes, so that the combined rate does not exceed the revenue-maximizing rate unless the primary objective is to reduce consumption drastically, not to raise revenue.
- In most European Union countries, a specific tax plus an ad valorem excise tax plus a VAT are applied on cigarettes. On alcoholic drinks, minimum excises per degree of alcohol (per liter) are mandated.

### Personal Income Tax

An attractive and elastic source of revenue, the personal income tax (PIT) may generate substantial revenue and promote equity, but it is hard to administer and therefore not a prominent source of revenue in LMICs:

- Revenue is elastic, so the PIT offers a stable source of revenue and helps to create an investment-friendly environment.
- The major advantage is that it can be designed to be progressive by applying higher tax rates on higher income brackets and thus follows the ability-to-pay principle and is more equitable.
- Measurement of income is often problematic, as the cost of earning income is deductible, and allowances and deductions are given for family members, medical expenses, and charitable contributions; all of this makes the PIT difficult to administer.

- Progressivity may be enhanced by changing the marginal tax rates or the zero-bracket threshold and by varying the size of tax brackets and marginal tax rates. However, the larger the number of brackets and the higher the marginal tax rates, the more complicated administration gets, which may promote evasion.
- Some countries—transition economies in particular—have chosen a flat-rate tax, which has advantages and disadvantages. A flat-tax rate is easier to administer, enhances compliance, and generates higher revenues, but it is less equitable, because most of the burden is borne by the middle class. Some countries apply different tax schedules to citizens and foreigners.
- There are two ways to apply the PIT: the global system, where all incomes are clubbed together, and the scheduler system, where tax rates vary by source of income. Both systems have pluses and minuses.
- For income tax to function properly, taxpayers' capacity and willingness to comply with the law are important.
- In the absence of a strong administration and lack of capacity of taxpayers to comply voluntarily, PIT seldom constitutes an important source of revenue in LMICs, where per capita income is low. PIT revenues come predominantly from withholding wages on public sector employees and workers in large enterprises.
- PIT may be focused only on large taxpayers and may look like an excise.
- In LMICs some major exceptions may erode the tax base: income from pension payments are taxed, while contributions to pensions are tax deductible; both employers and employees contribute to the social insurance fund, but contributions to the fund are tax deductible, while payments to the beneficiary are tax exempt; capital gains are ignored; contributions to life insurance are tax deductible, but payments to beneficiaries are tax exempt; sometimes lottery winnings are tax exempt; fringe benefits to government employees are effectively untaxed; and legal provision are not applied.

### Corporate Income Tax

The corporate income tax (CIT) is imposed on the net profits of a company. Income from all sources, including business, trading, and nonbusiness, are included in the base:

- Deductions are allowed for the cost of goods sold, depreciation of capital assets, financing costs, and overhead.
- Tax rates may vary considerably; top CIT tax rates have been declining over the years due to tax competition, as capital is internationally mobile.
- For the same reason, capital is often taxed lightly compared with labor, and the CIT tax rate is usually kept below the highest marginal tax rate under PIT.
- Most countries have a single CIT rate, but some have lower rates on some sectors, particularly small taxpayers, or some regions. Some countries apply a higher rate on natural resources like minerals, oil, and gas.

- Foreign companies, including branches, pay income tax at the normal CIT rate but often also an additional withholding tax on repatriated profits. Sometimes different tax rates are imposed on subsidiaries and branches.
- Depreciation rules should be as close to economic depreciation as possible.
- Most countries have loss offset, loss carry-forward, and loss carry-backward provisions.
- Tax incentives seldom work, but are still prevalent in LMICs.
- Tax holidays are absent in high-income countries, but they are still prevalent in LMICs due to regional tax competition.
- Tax expenditure analysis as part of the budgeting process may help to eliminate excessive and outdated incentives or exemptions.
- The issue of transfer pricing is particularly relevant in the case of multinational companies. Many LMICs lack a dedicated unit in the ministry of finance, tax department, or revenue authority and have only cursory legal and administrative provisions for dealing with transfer pricing. Also, an asymmetry of capacity exists vis-à-vis big corporations, both domestic and transnational, although several models, including the Organisation for Economic Co-operation and Development model, are available for transfer pricing laws and rules.
- Finally, integration of the PIT and CIT should be considered, and some partial integration is generally adopted.

## Assessing the Tax Administration

The tax administration administers tax laws and related legislation. It has been rightly said that tax policy is tax administration: tax administration determines how tax policy gets implemented. Broadly, tax policy determines the objectives or functions of revenue collection, including both inland or domestic taxes and customs duties comprising import and export taxes and also the import component of the goods and services tax, VAT, and excise, which plays an important role in resource mobilization, particularly in low-income countries. Tax administration is also responsible for collecting other earmarked taxes, fees, and other special-purpose funds, such as social security contributions (pensions, disability, health, unemployment) and road maintenance levies.

Tax administration also performs other functions that are vital to the economy. For instance, the customs or border tax administration ensures border control, security, safety, health, and environmental standards enforcement. It also facilitates trade and business in conjunction with the administration of ports and transport as well as the administration of exemptions and incentive programs that are bonded or zone based. Similarly, domestic or internal tax administration is responsible for registration and administration of exempt sectors (diplomatic privileges, nongovernmental organizations, charitable organizations) and for domestic tax expenditures arising out of sector tax incentives for employment or investment.

Before adopting advanced instruments of taxation and modernizing the tax system, the traditional functions of the tax administration should be diagnosed to determine whether the fundamentals are sound. The component functions of the tax administration depend on the degree of self versus agency assessment— that is, taxpayer active versus passive administration. Several basic elements of tax administration have to be in place, as discussed next.

### Assessment of Tax Liability

The following are the necessary components of assessment, the starting point in tax administration:

- Taxpayer identification and registration
- Tax accounting to assess tax liability
- Legal interpretation of tax provisions
- Enforcement of registration and filing of tax returns (stop filers, people in the system who do not pay)
- Appeals against registration or assessment determinations
- Education and taxpayer services.

### Collections

The collection function entails the following:

- Receiving current payments
- Receiving arrears
- Accounting for receipts and arrears (unpaid liabilities), including penalties and interest
- Enforcing arrears or debt collections by administrative or legal instruments
- Handling appeals against penalties or enforcement actions
- Providing education and taxpayer services.

### The Audit Function

The tax administration should have both an internal and an external audit system in place. The internal audit is undertaken to ensure compliance with the integrity and efficiency of administrative systems and procedures; it includes internal investigations and compliance with efficiency measures. The external audit is undertaken to ensure taxpayer compliance and is of two types: desk audits, which are confined to checking returns against available data, such as third-party information, and field audits, which are more detailed, comprehensive, or targeted.

External audits are undertaken to ensure that financial accounts comply with tax laws. They have the following components:

- Intelligence, inspections, and investigations
- Enforcement of audit findings
- Appeals against fines, penalties, or enforcement actions.

### Dispute Resolution

Disputes are bound to arise at different levels of tax administration: assessment, collections, and audit. Thus, a dispute resolution mechanism is needed and is an important part of customer-focused administration. The cost-efficient system is generally two stages:

- Administrative or departmental review by officials somewhat distanced from the process that caused the dispute
- Special tax courts or judicial courts of law.

Most countries use some combination of these.

# Tax Project Data Analysis

Subhash Nepali and Steven B. Webb

This appendix examines the work that the World Bank has done on revenue policy and administration, how the work is combined into country programs, and how the different types of country programs correlate with improved tax efficiency and higher tax revenue as a share of gross domestic product (GDP).

Bank support for improving countries' tax policy and administration comes in many forms, including development policy loans (DPLs); investment and technical assistance loans; analytical and advisory activities (AAAs), including economic and sector work and nonlending technical assistance by the Bank; and advisory services by the International Finance Corporation (IFC).

To create a database for statistical analysis, we started with the 650 Bank projects—loans, AAAs, advisory services, and others—that had tax components identified in the Business Warehouse and that closed between 1999 and 2014. We narrowed this list to include only lending projects with at least 15 percent tax components and AAAs and advisory services with at least 25 percent tax components. These selection criteria yielded 254 projects implemented in 96 countries. We checked this list with leading Bank tax specialists.

Many countries had more than one tax project, and these projects typically overlapped in time, making it impossible to associate individual projects with changes in aggregate indicators of tax policy and administration. Also, most tax experts said that the most important issue was to determine the mix of Bank assistance related to taxes that was most associated with success. The renewed effort to coordinate across the Taxation Thematic Group also favored comparing different programs of Bank assistance in an integrated way.

## Categories of Programs

Using four standard operational categories of projects—investment and technical assistance loans; DPLs, including sector adjustment loans and sectoral adjustment loans; World Bank AAAs (economic and sector work and nonlending technical assistance); and IFC AAAs (for example, business taxation advisory services)—led to 14 program combinations, with a distribution of projects and countries, as shown in table C.1.[1] Most of the projects were part of programs with more than one type of project. The countries with multifaceted programs were a minority, however, as most of the 96 countries with some tax program received only one kind of assistance: only DPL, only investment lending, or only AAAs.

These programs were not assigned to countries in a random manner. Rather, they were the outcome of dialogue between Bank representatives and government counterparts. Thus, much of the choice about the type of assistance reflects what assistance the government agreed to and perhaps was enthusiastic to receive, although the degree of enthusiasm may have varied. The extent to which the initial idea for the activity came from the government or the Bank varied. Our data do not reveal whether, over time, the country (especially the ministry of finance and the tax administration agency) increased its understanding and appreciation of what Bank support would bring.

Therefore, the tax program of a country is not an independent variable that caused the observed outcome. In addition, countries received assistance on tax matters from sources other than the World Bank, including the International Monetary Fund (IMF), the Organisation for Economic Co-Operation and Development, bilateral assistance, and so on.

**Table C.1  Number of Countries and Projects Receiving World Bank Assistance on Taxation**

| Tax program (mutually exclusive categories) | Countries | Projects |
|---|---|---|
| IL only | 7 | 7 |
| DPL only | 16 | 23 |
| IL and DPL | 6 | 18 |
| WB AAAs (no lending) | 23 | 45 |
| IFC AAAs | 12 | 14 |
| WB AAAs and IFC AAAs | 2 | 6 |
| IL and WB AAAs | 2 | 4 |
| IL and IFC AAAs | 1 | 2 |
| DPL and WB AAAs | 6 | 22 |
| DPL and IFC AAAs | 4 | 11 |
| IL and WB AAAs and IFC AAAs | 2 | 6 |
| PL and WB AAAs and IFC AAAs | 4 | 22 |
| IL and DPL and IFC AAAs | 7 | 46 |
| IL and DPL and WB AAAs and IFC AAAs | 4 | 28 |
| Total | 96 | 254 |

*Note:* AAAs = analytical and advisory activities; DPL = development policy lending; IFC = International Finance Corporation; IL = investment lending; PL = policy lending; WB = World Bank.

## Outcomes

The analysis presented in table C.2 uses two indicators of countries' tax performance:

- Change in tax revenue as a share of GDP
- Country Policy and Institutional Assessment (CPIA) rating for CPIA 14: Efficiency of Revenue Mobilization.

For each country, we examined the change in the indicator from the beginning to the end of the program with tax projects that the country had with the Bank. The analysis compares revenue collection and efficiency before the project with revenue collection and efficiency after the project. As far as possible, we picked data from a year before the tax project started and a year after the tax project ended. The start date was selected from the years when the Bank started implementation (the first project in one country, where multiple projects were implemented) in a time frame between 1999 and 2015. Similarly, the end date was chosen from the years when the tax project was concluded in the country (year for the last concluded project in case multiple projects existed in a country). This exercise considered only closed projects.

For tax revenue as a share of GDP, we used the latest IMF, Fiscal Affairs Department Revenue Panel Database.[2] These data were available for the years up to 2013. Therefore, we used the values from 2013 for the end point of tax programs that ended in 2013, 2014, and 2015.

For revenue efficiency, we used CPIA 14 data, which were available for 1999 and for the years from 2004 to 2013. We used the data values from 1999 for programs starting in the years from 2000 to 2003. Similarly, we used the CPIA values from 2013 for 2014 and 2015.[3]

**Table C.2  Countries' Tax Performance Corresponding to World Bank Tax Program**
*Number of countries in each category, unless otherwise noted*

| | CPIA 14 taxation efficiency | | | Tax revenue as % of GDP | | |
|---|---|---|---|---|---|---|
| Tax program | Improved | Declined | No change | Average % change | Increased | Declined |
| DPL and IL and AAAs | 9 | 1 | 1 | 2.09 | 8 | 3 |
| IL only | 5 | 0 | 2 | 2.22 | 5 | 1 |
| IL and DPL | 4 | 0 | 2 | 1.20 | 3 | 2 |
| IL and AAAs (WB and IFC, combined) | 4 | 0 | 1 | 1.85 | 3 | 1 |
| DPL only | 5 | 0 | 10 | 0.80 | 6 | 7 |
| DPL and AAAs (WB and IFC, combined) | 8 | 2 | 4 | 1.66 | 11 | 3 |
| AAAs only | 11 | 2 | 21 | 0.69 | 17 | 17 |

*Note:* AAAs = analytical and advisory activities; CPIA = Country Policy and Institutional Assessment; DPL = development policy lending; GDP = gross domestic product; IFC = International Finance Corporation; IL = investment lending; WB = World Bank.

It is reassuring, but not surprising, that almost all countries receiving World Bank taxation assistance through DPLs, investment loans, and AAAs showed improvement on both measures of tax performance (table C.3).

The critical ingredient in successful tax programs was investment lending. The outcomes from programs with investment lending only, with investment lending in combination with DPL, and with investment lending in combination with AAAs all showed positive results on both indicators. This result is consistent with the finding of the Independent Evaluation Group's evaluation of public sector reform, which found that tax administration reform was the most successful of the four areas of Bank support for public sector reform (IEG 2008). Improving tax performance in both institutional and fiscal dimensions does not happen quickly or without deep engagement and commitment. Investment loans for tax improvement—which generally focus on administration—typically take five years or more. DPLs and AAAs with tax components have much shorter duration and require less engagement from a country's tax officials.

Tax programs with only DPLs performed the worst. Two-thirds of the countries with only tax-related DPLs showed no improvement in CPIA 14, and the majority experienced declines in tax revenue as a share of GDP. Since DPLs provide untied fiscal resources, a government might choose to avoid the political cost of raising more tax revenue. Having AAAs in the program along with a

**Table C.3  Number of Tax Programs for IDA and IBRD (and Blend) Countries**

| Tax program | IDA | | IBRD | |
|---|---|---|---|---|
| | Countries | Projects | Countries | Projects |
| IL | 3 | 3 | 4 | 4 |
| PL | 8 | 11 | 8 | 12 |
| IL and PL | 2 | 4 | 4 | 14 |
| WB AAAs | 8 | 9 | 15 | 36 |
| IFC AAAs | 9 | 9 | 3 | 5 |
| WB AAAs and IFC AAAs | 1 | 4 | 1 | 2 |
| IL and WB AAAs | 2 | 4 | 0 | 0 |
| IL and IFC AAAs | 1 | 2 | 0 | 0 |
| PL and WB AAAs | 1 | 4 | 5 | 18 |
| PL and IFC AAAs | 3 | 9 | 1 | 2 |
| IL and WB AAAs and IFC AAAs | 2 | 6 | 0 | 0 |
| PL and WB AAAs and IFC AAAs | 3 | 14 | 1 | 8 |
| IL and PL and IFC AAAs | 1 | 4 | 6 | 42 |
| IL and PL and WB AAAs and IFC AAAs | 2 | 14 | 2 | 14 |
| Total | 46 | 97 | 50 | 157 |

*Note:* AAAs = analytical and advisory activities; IBRD = International Bank for Reconstruction and Development; IDA = International Development Agency; IFC = International Finance Corporation; IL = investment lending; PL = policy lending; WB = World Bank.

DPL corresponds to more positive outcomes, perhaps because of the greater duration and institutional depth of the engagement.

Having a tax program with AAAs and no lending corresponded to no change on average. Only a third of countries with such programs had improved CPIA scores, and tax revenue declined as often as it increased. IFC advisory services alone had somewhat better outcomes on average. World Bank AAAs with no lending had poorer average outcomes.

## Notes

1. The distinction between International Development Agency countries and International Bank for Reconstruction and Development (and blend) countries is presented in table C.3.

2. For revenue as a percentage of GDP for IMF countries, see IMF, Fiscal Affairs Department, Tax Policy Division, updated Revenue Panel Database, December 18, 2014.

3. Results with the CPIA data are only reported for averages of at least five countries because the data on individual International Bank for Reconstruction and Development countries are confidential.

## Reference

IEG (Independent Evaluation Group). 2008. *Public Sector Reform: What Works and Why*. Washington, DC: World Bank.

APPENDIX D

# Resource Mobilization: Lessons Learned from Select World Bank Tax Administration Reform Activities

Individuals think of taxes as inevitable, but to be avoided as much as possible. However, reducing poverty and promoting prosperity for a society require raising resources to finance appropriate public spending on social services and economic infrastructure. This process starts with tax policy and law, but the objectives of tax policy cannot be achieved without adequate tax administration. Some experts put it even more strongly: "Tax administration is tax policy" (Bird and Casanegra de Jantscher 1992). In other words, what actually happens in terms of revenue collected and distribution of the tax burden depends as much on how the tax law is administered as on the provisions in the law itself. Much of the shortfall in revenue and inequity in tax burden results from inefficient or corrupt administration of the tax law on the books. Furthermore, tax policy reforms may be blocked politically if politicians, voters, and interest groups question the need for tax reform (for example, to broaden the tax base in Mexico in 2001) because the tax administration is not even collecting the taxes already on the books.

This appendix considers the two main phases of a tax reform project: preparation (diagnosis and design) and implementation (bidding packages, performance indicators). Then it looks at issues arising from the context of the borrower and the context within the World Bank Group. The concluding section offers some suggestions for how to strengthen the business model for the Bank's work on taxation issues. Throughout, it uses evidence from interviews and project documents concerning a limited number of tax administration loans (some of which are described in box D.1). Appendix C provides a statistical analysis of the characteristics of projects with substantial tax policy and administration components that closed between 1999 and 2014.

## Box D.1  Sample of World Bank Tax Projects

### Bulgaria: Revenue Administration Reform Project
**US$26.8 million disbursed, 2003–09**

In the course of transition to a market economy, Bulgaria sought to strengthen its revenue administration. The project addressed gaps in management, human resources, business processes, and information technology (IT) systems identified in a joint International Monetary Fund (IMF)–World Bank mission. The main objective was to establish an economically efficient, sustainable public revenue collection system that facilitates private sector development and complies with the requirements for European Union (EU) accession.

Project objectives were achieved, and the results exceeded expectations. The Ministry of Finance executed a change management plan to establish the National Revenue Authority (NRA). Strong coordination between donors resulted in complementarity—the IMF provided technical assistance for the legal framework, and the EU supported the NRA call center. Improvements in voluntary tax compliance and increased efficiency in revenue collection created the basis for Bulgaria to reduce its tax and social contribution rates and become a competitive investment location in the region. Lower tax and social security rates helped to reduce the share of the informal economy by 30 percent between 2002 and 2008.

### Colombia: Public Financial Management Project II
**US$35.31 million disbursed, 2000–09**

This project was designed in 1998, when Colombia was suffering the effects of a sharp economic recession due to low oil and coffee prices and limited availability of international finance. To address a rising deficit, the government requested a three-year extended fund facility from the IMF. To implement the public financial management reforms targeted under this program, authorities requested World Bank support to reinforce the institutional capacity of the tax and customs administration and strengthen public expenditure management at the central government level.

High-level commitment supported the achievement of project objectives. The initiative made a substantial contribution toward improving Colombia's revenue performance with regard to increasing tax revenues, decreasing the tax compliance gap and contraband, and improving the efficiency of the tax and customs administration, as measured by the cost-of-collection ratio. Colombia now has a modern, high-performing tax administration. Its management system is comprehensive, its structure and systems are closely aligned with agency and national goals, and its performance ranks with the best in the Latin American region.

### Guatemala: Tax Administration Technical Assistance Loan
**US$19.3 million disbursed, 1997–2007**

With one of the lowest tax revenue ratios in Latin America—8.8 percent of gross domestic product (GDP) in 1996—Guatemala's historically weak revenue performance was a crucial factor undermining the country's macroeconomic performance as well as its overall development prospects. Specifically, wide annual variations in tax collection threatened public account balances and subjected public investment to disruptive cycles of "stop-go" spending. In addition, low tax revenues severely constrained public investment and social sector

*box continues next page*

**Box D.1  Sample of World Bank Tax Projects** *(continued)*

spending, limiting poverty alleviation efforts. To address these challenges, this project sought to improve the effectiveness and efficiency of tax and customs administration and to increase tax revenues.

Political support for the project was uneven. Legislation to create a new tax administration structure led to an initial one-year delay in project implementation in 1997 and further delays in 2002, when political conditions were not supportive and budgetary resources were not allocated to the tax administration. Despite the obstacles and challenges faced during implementation, the operation made a substantial contribution toward improving Guatemala's revenue performance by supporting the creation of a new tax agency for internal revenue and customs with operational, financial, and human resource management autonomy. Targets took longer to reach than anticipated. However, by 2006, net tax revenues reached 10.3 percent of GDP.

**Pakistan: Tax Administration Reform Project**
**US$48.41 million disbursed, 2004–11**

To address a low rate of revenue mobilization (10–13 percent of GDP), Pakistan targeted tax policy and administration reforms to (a) improve the effectiveness, responsiveness, efficiency, integrity, and fairness of tax administration; (b) promote compliance with tax laws and broaden the tax base; and (c) promote trade facilitation.

Results from the project did not meet expectations, although moderate progress was made in increasing the tax base and expanding the tax registry. At the time of the project, tax reform was not high on the government's policy agenda, and the project encountered strong internal resistance to change. Inadequate technical assistance was provided prior to implementation, and the project did not have an adequate local presence. Tax policy reform was not sequenced with tax administration, and consensus was not reached on implementation of a new IT system. While the objectives of this project were not met, lessons were incorporated into programming that is currently under way.

## Preparation: Diagnosis and Design

### Diagnosis

Good diagnosis is clearly a prerequisite for successful revenue administration reform, and the World Bank Group has provided diagnostic services in several forms and sometimes has relied on diagnosis done by others, particularly the International Monetary Fund. The diagnosis may be done as a self-standing product or as a guide for designing a lending operation to support tax administration reform. A diagnosis that is foreseen as the basis for a probable lending project usually pays more attention to the information system and to personnel reorganization and training, which are costly elements that the loan can help to finance.

Which organization does the diagnosis also matters, as this decision affects the prioritization of objectives. When the International Monetary Fund (IMF) does the diagnosis, the primary objective is usually to raise more revenue, in order to close a fiscal gap or to create more fiscal space. When (prior to the latest reorganization) the International Finance Corporation (IFC) does the diagnosis through its advisory services facility, the emphasis is on making private business invest-ment more attractive—streamlined processes for filing and payment, less corrup-tion, and the like—but with indeterminate effects on government revenue.[1] When Poverty Reduction and Economic Management (PREM) units for economic policy or public sector lead the diagnosis, the balance of objectives varies among raising revenue, promoting private sector investment, and reducing corruption. One intention of bringing all of the Bank's work on taxes within the new community of practice for taxation is to ensure that the objectives of the work across the World Bank Group are aligned with the overall needs of the country involved and not driven by the inclinations of the particular unit initiat-ing and doing the work.

The IFC's advisory services on business taxation grew large in the last two decades, compared with the World Bank—the International Bank for Reconstruction and Development and the International Development Association—nonlending technical assistance (NLTA) on taxes, and had a different funding model. The Bank work was often seen as supporting potential projects, which later generate a return through the lending. In Guatemala, the NLTA on tax administration helped to bring a tax administration reform project (TARP) into the project pipeline. The IFC's business taxation advisory services were not linked with projects and received funding through trust funds and some client co-financing in the case of middle-income countries. Harmonizing the funding models is one of the challenges facing the World Bank Group since the reorganization into Global Practices.

### Link to Reform of Tax Policy Law
Tax policy and tax administration work symbiotically. As noted, the actual work-ing of the tax law depends a lot on how it is administered, especially in countries with weak and uncertain rule of law. Also, improvement of tax administration often requires revised policies and procedural authority in the law. Efficient col-lection and administration of the value added tax (VAT) and income taxes, in particular, need policy reforms to eliminate exemptions (and zero-rating clauses) and simplify complex rate structures, which otherwise become avenues for eva-sion and make tax calculations more difficult even for honest payers. Many countries in Europe and Central Asia, where most personal income tax (PIT) was reported and paid by employers and collected by withholding from pay-checks, found that moving to a single flat-rate tax improved total revenue collection. There remained challenges to getting a fair share of revenue from self-employed professionals, "small" business owners, and other self-employed. The political economy of doing so could become easier, however, once a large number of workers have to pay the PIT. In Pakistan, the failure to change tax policy contributed to the failure of reform on the administrative side, while in Bulgaria and Mexico, the revisions of policy law contributed to the success of administrative reform.

Changes in the law concerning tax bases and tax rates are not enough. Successful administration reform usually requires regulatory changes in the law, giving the tax agency the authority to conduct inspections, accept electronic filing and payment, make electronic payment of refunds, get data from banks, and take other steps not envisioned or permitted in the laws from the past century. Pakistan's TARP failed because (among several reasons) the government did not make such regulatory changes, and the Bank team preparing the project did not guide the government through these steps or did not plan the project with time to do them. The necessary preparation entails more than just drafting new legislation; it also requires stakeholder consultations to work out the details with the public and private sector actors involved. Such consultations can reveal the need for clarifications in tax legislation and harmonization between the legislation and implementing regulations. The Russian Federation's Transitional Assistance Management Program (TAMP) II and Tanzania's Tax Administration Project are examples of doing this well. Without such attention to detail, even conceptually excellent reforms will not achieve their objectives.

### Scope of Revenue Administration Reform

Revenue administration reform projects, studies, and NLTA vary in how much of the public sector revenue flow they cover. The core concern of a TARP is almost always internal revenue collected by the national government, and the decision regarding how far to go beyond that depends on the country's institutional circumstances.

Even internal revenue sometimes starts out divided by type of tax—income tax, VAT, excises, and so on—and in those cases, it takes some time and consultation to bring the stakeholders on board. Failure to do so contributed to the overall failure in Pakistan. In Vietnam, a new law for the PIT, essentially separating it from the rest of inland revenue, led to the failure of the TARP. Taking a consolidated approach to inland revenue has major advantages that usually make the effort worthwhile:

- Information gathered for one tax helps to detect when there is evasion or misreporting on another. For instance, a large volume of sales reported for the VAT would imply that there should be a corresponding amount of taxable corporate income and withholding of PIT for employees.
- Reporting and filing to a consolidated agency can help business taxpayers to pay all of their taxes due in the most efficient way.
- Audits can be more thorough and yield more additional revenue if they are done for all taxes at once.

The successful TARPs reviewed here initially or in the course of the project organized the revenue administration by function—reporting, collection, audit, and so forth—rather than by tax. Several of the failed projects showed, however, that this consolidation was not quick or easy and that the projects needed to factor in enough time and resources to work the changes through with stakeholders in the tax agency and in the private sector. In Pakistan, the hurried and underprepared attempt to reorganize the tax agency according to function (rather than by tax) contributed to the failure of the TARP. South Asian countries have a long tradition of separate administrations and personnel for major inland taxes—income, sales, VAT, excises—which dates back to colonial British regimes. In such situations, reorganization by function needs long-term, in-depth preparation.

Almost all tax systems have special regimes for small taxpayers—small enterprises, including self-employed. With the rationale of making the tax burden progressive, the effective tax rate of the small-payer regime is usually lower than the combination of VAT, corporate income tax (CIT), and the PIT that it more or less replaces. Consequently, mid-size and even some large enterprises will try to present themselves or even reorganize themselves to qualify for the small-payer regime.[2] Although this problem originates in tax policy law and much of the solution must come ultimately from policy reforms, the immediate challenge lands on the revenue administration agency.

Key decisions for designing revenue administration reform are whether to include customs and how much to integrate customs administration with inland revenue. The administrations of both generally need reform, but whether to combine them depends on the institutional setting in the country. There are several advantages to unifying the accounts and information systems. Having single enterprise accounts for customs and inland revenue helps to prevent rebates from going to overall tax debtors. Good export and import data are essential for assessing the VAT correctly. Customs data can also help to identify large business activity that should be yielding VAT and income tax revenue. In Colombia and Guatemala, unification was useful in these ways.

Unifying the customs administration with inland revenue has some disadvantages, however. It adds complexity and has only worked well when agencies have the capacity to deal with it. Inland revenue and customs administration staff have different cultures and attitudes, including toward corruption. Design of the project should face these issues squarely. In Bulgaria, a factor in the success of the TARP was the decision to reform inland revenue only, to stay focused, and to avoid mixing in the more corrupt elements from the customs side. In Mexico, the TARP initially included customs reform, but that component received little attention during project preparation and was dropped early in implementation, in order to minimize the complexity of an already complex project.

Most countries, especially large ones, have subnational governments with some taxing authority. Although some places have realized economies by having the national agency collect some subnational taxes, as with Revenue Canada, the successful TARPs at the Bank have not pursued such consolidation.[3] The TARP in Bulgaria devolved to local governments the collection of local fees and small taxes, because they were a fiscally unrewarding distraction for the national tax agency. This change contributed to the project's success. In Mexico, some of the state governments have provided technical assistance to municipal governments in doing cadasters for the property tax—with support from a development policy loan (DPL) in the case of the State of Mexico.

Sometimes, where there is adequate capacity in the bureaucracy, it makes sense to reform tax administration as part of a broader project to strengthen public financial management, for example, including revenue forecasting and expenditure management, as in Colombia. In Mexico, the TARP helped to open the door for a separate project (on a fee-for-service basis) to improve expenditure management, including back-office information technology (IT) for the Treasury and Undersecretariat of Finance for Expenditure. This information system was intended to share information with the tax administration system, but it faced opposition from other parts of the ministry and was not implemented. In Jamaica in the mid-1990s, initially there was discussion of undertaking tax administration reform as part of a broad public sector reform project, but difficulties encountered at the design stage led the (reconstituted) team to take a more modest approach—a simple TARP and then an agency-by-agency reform process elsewhere in the public sector.[4]

## Mix of Components
Once the government and the Bank team have decided which revenue streams to cover, they need to agree on the scope of activities to undertake in the project. Again, there is no one right answer or right size; the approach should depend on the needs, ambitiousness, and capacity of the government and its revenue agency. Eight common features to consider are IT, process rationalization, personnel system reform, large taxpayer unit, small taxpayer and informal sector unit, capacity building for transfer pricing issues, office remodeling and construction, and taxpayer service and outreach.

### Information Technology
NLTA often has extensive recommendations about what to do with IT. Moving from manual to IT processes offers many potential advantages: faster processing, lower labor costs, automatic and more accurate record keeping, fewer opportunities for bribes and corruption, and so on. The challenge is to make the IT investment in a cost-efficient way and to do the many complementary reforms necessary for the IT investment to have the desired effect. Making cost-efficient IT investments includes, for example, having adaptability in the program to take advantage of improvements that are sure to become available in IT products. The main complementary reforms—essential for making good use of the new hardware and software—are listed as usual components of a TARP.

### Rationalization of Processes and Reallocation of Effort within the Revenue Agency
Even without (new) IT, some process rationalization is worthwhile, and other process changes are needed to implement automated data handling. As more filing and payment collection are handled by digital automation, more resources are freed up and should go to auditing, identification of nonfilers, and collection of arrears. Typical programs also integrate filing, revenue collection, auditing, and record keeping for different taxes—reorganization by function, which has the benefits and caveats discussed in the section on scope.

### Strategic Planning and Management in the Tax Headquarters
As the list of "important" activities grows, management at the center needs stronger capacity to identify the priorities and proper sequencing and to monitor what

is happening in the agency. It needs capacity for collecting and analyzing data on the agency's performance and for identifying risks. This capacity does not happen automatically or without cost; better projects have a component to address capacity building. For example, Bulgaria's TARP supported capacity building to analyze compliance levels and compliance trends for major taxes, economic activities, and business segments. It also included development of policy analysis capacity and introduction of compliance studies. Risk-based audit selection was a key element in Kazakhstan's TARP.

### Personnel System Reform

To implement process reforms, the need for some jobs expands (auditors, programmers) and the need for others contracts (collection agents, clerks). To some extent, staff can be retrained to move from declining job areas to expanding ones, but the necessary skills and aptitudes often differ too much for this method to address most of the necessary change. Retrenchment and new hiring are often necessary, and the two processes rarely move at the same pace. Both relocating existing personnel and bringing on new hires require substantial training of personnel. Project design and the anticipated implementation timetable have to take this need into account.

Considering these changes can heighten awareness of the need for wider reform in the civil service and other government personnel systems. Notions of economies of scale and the Bank's administrative restrictions on the number of projects per country sometimes make project and country teams inclined to combine tax administration reform with wider reforms of personnel systems. This has worked in practice only when the government was already prepared and committed to undertake civil service reform, as was the case in Bulgaria. There and in Guatemala, essentially all personnel of the tax administration were fired, and a new cadre of personnel was hired under the auspices of an outside agent— the U.K. Department for International Development in Bulgaria and Price-Waterhouse in Guatemala. In Indonesia, the government's simultaneous actions to reform the civil service contributed to failure of the TARP, even though the projects were nominally separate. In Pakistan, an attempt to do an extreme reorganization of personnel, as part of the functional organization of the revenue agency, failed and contributed to failure of the whole TARP.

### Large Taxpayer Unit

Most TARPs include the creation or strengthening of special administrative sections and rules for large taxpayers. Creating or strengthening the large taxpayer unit (LTU) has usually proven a cost-effective way to increase revenue collection, because large payers are the likely source of most of the revenue increases and small payers figure that they have a right to evade paying taxes if big companies are not paying theirs. LTUs figured prominently in the success of TARPs in Colombia, Jamaica, and Mexico. Unless there is a clear reason to the contrary, an LTU should be part of any TARP. To sustain the success of reform, the enhanced reporting and scrutiny of the large payer regime needs to increase its coverage steadily—lowering the threshold for inclusion—to avoid encouraging firms to pretend not to be large.

### Measures to Bring Small Payers and Informal Sector into the Tax Net

The special regimes for small payers and the persistent efforts of enterprises in the informal sector to stay out of the tax net pose challenges for every revenue agency. No good solution has been found, although the large number of potential payers makes the informal sector an attractive target. Some reform of tax policy law is usually needed. The TARPs that have tried to deal with this issue have had mixed success. The measures generate substantial political opposition, due to the large number of people affected. They usually generate little revenue in the short and medium term, although some former Soviet countries, like Georgia, have had success.

### Building Capacity to Deal with Transfer Pricing and Profit Shifting

As countries engage more closely with the world economy and corporate profit taxes become potentially more important sources of revenue, tax authorities need to prevent companies from evading taxes through bookkeeping tricks that shift profits abroad where firms face lower taxes. The most common vehicle for this is transfer pricing, by which the in-country branch of a firm books inflated prices for inputs it buys from an overseas branch or underprices the output it sells to an overseas affiliate. Setting rules for determining transfer prices can deal with this problem. Often the rules are built into treaties or contracts between the firm and tax authorities in the country and abroad, like European countries or the United States. Arranging such transfer pricing agreements takes substantial technical expertise, and enforcing them takes even more. The IFC's advisory services for business taxation has been the most active part of the World Bank Group on this issue. If the country does a lot of trade in half-finished to finished manufactured goods and the revenue authority has adequate technical capacity, it is worthwhile for a TARP to have a component to improve transfer pricing and profit shifting. In Colombia, conditions were appropriate, and the TARP had a successful component to improve the country's transfer pricing arrangements. In Bulgaria, the issues seemed too complex to undertake, and keeping the project focused on the basics contributed to its success.

### Office Remodeling

Many Bank-supported TARPs have substantial components—often a quarter or more of total cost—for upgrading or rebuilding offices. This might be a worthwhile activity—making employees more productive and taxpayers more comfortable—but it is rarely as high a priority as other components and may distract from them. Designers of the TARP should ask the following questions: To what extent is office remodeling essential for improving revenue administration? Is it mainly intended to increase the volume of lending and to sweeten incentives for revenue administration officials? In Bulgaria, problems with the bidding for a new building—included in the original project—led to the decision to drop the project component for the building. This had no adverse effect on the project's overall success and saved the government money, as it found less expensive alternatives.

### Taxpayer Service and Outreach

Helping taxpayers to get the information they need to comply with the tax code generally has had good results. Russia's TAMP II provides a good example. It requires conscious efforts to change traditional attitudes and culture in the tax agency.

## Implementation

Three of the issues in implementing TARPs are whether to develop custom systems or use off-the-shelf packages, how to organize the bidding for different parts of the project, and how to measure the progress of the project and its success relative to its intended outcomes.

### Custom or Off-the-Shelf?

The initial assessment of the revenue system should indicate whether the existing systems (revenue management, auditing, record storage, personnel management) are good enough to upgrade and, if they are, with which systems or whether the entire system should be replaced. Upgrading a system, whether an initially custom system or a conglomeration of standard subsystems, would require an essentially custom job. To replace the whole system, an off-the-shelf product is usually better. A good standard package will have fewer bugs, have better documentation, and be easier to upgrade in the future.

In Mexico's TARP, after quickly discarding the initial plan to have an essentially custom system assembled from a large number of custom and off-the-shelf components, the Tax Administration Service (Servicio de Administración Tributaria, or SAT) and Bank teams agreed on buying a complete package from Oracle (PeopleSoft). At the time (2002–03), however, government resource planning tools for tax administration application were not yet fully developed. Hence, the purchased package required considerable customization to make it work in the Mexican context. Now several good integrated packages are available on the market. Even Finland and New Zealand, which have two of the best tax administrations in the world, have replaced their multiple systems (more than 100 in Finland) with off-the-shelf integrated systems for revenue management.[5]

### Organization of the Bidding

Very different components—like IT and office remodeling—usually need to have separate bidding packages. For the IT component(s), the unified bidding issue is less clear.

Having one big package for all the IT components offers the apparent advantage of integrating all the data systems. In Mexico, the TARP used a single large bidding package for the whole project, and this proved to be advantageous, because extreme fragmentation of the SAT was a central problem that the project aimed to address.[6] In most cases, however, a single bidding package for

IT has proven problematic, contributing substantially to failure of the TARPs in Indonesia and Vietnam.

Organizing all of IT into one big package takes longer than doing the first of several smaller packages and delays the start of the whole project. In any case, it is important to start preparing the IT procurement as soon as possible, even before the project is officially begun. Not all parts of the IT system can be used immediately, and if all are bid at the same time, then some parts may be technologically somewhat obsolete two years or so later when they are actually used. Having three or four IT procurement packages with different specialized firms and just-in-time procurement probably works best. For instance, it is possible to separate the revenue management system, the servers and database hardware, and the telecommunications system. In terms of political economy, a project with several components has the potential advantage of attracting several champions in the revenue administration, making it less vulnerable to the departure or downfall of a single champion.

When countries do such divided procurement, they either need to have the in-house technical capacity in the revenue agency to coordinate the different parts or they need to contract for such coordination. For instance, the Bulgaria TARP had divided procurement, and the revenue authority had enough technical capacity to do the integration. In Romania, there is less technical expertise, and the TARP will have to have an additional procurement package to outsource the integration tasks to a specialist contractor.

Also, avoiding a large number of small bidding packages is preferable for several reasons. It is hard to coordinate contractors doing different components. Even doing all of the separate bids when there are dozens of separate components may take excessive time and gives up potential bargaining leverage. Safeguards against corruption lose their effectiveness when there are too many bids to monitor—creating opportunities for petty corruption. In the initial design of Mexico's TARP, there was excessive fragmentation of the bidding packages, but they were consolidated before the solicitation for bids began.

### Coordinating Implementation with the Private Sector

There are two ways to obtain private sector involvement and support for a reform project. One approach is to involve the private sector in the project steering committee. This happened in Kazakhstan, according to the project appraisal document. The Bulgaria project also included a consultative forum with external members, as did an early Pakistan project. The second approach is to include project activities to improve cooperation with the private sector, in particular, taxpayer associations and tax intermediaries. Russia's TAMP II took such an approach.

### Project Development Objectives and Intermediate Indicators

To indicate whether the project is designed and implemented properly, the project development objectives and intermediate indicators should focus on what is under the control of the implementing agency—typically the revenue agency, which is under the ministry of finance (box D.2).

---

**Box D.2  Which Program Development Objectives and Intermediate Indicators Were Potentially Suitable for the Program for Results Design?**

Tax administration reform projects are candidates for using the Program for Results design. One obvious application is to use the recommended revisions to the tax law and to the procedural code as benchmarks (conditions) for moving ahead with procurement of the investments.

---

Examples of good targets are the number of late filers of CIT and VAT for large and medium enterprises; number of audits; number of audit adjustments and amount collected from them; average number of days to process a VAT refund; and percentage of returns filed electronically.

A common indicator is revenue collection as a share of GDP. For good reasons, this indicator is not popular with revenue agencies, because revenue collection results from many things beyond the control of the agency. In some cases, as in Vietnam, aggressive tax policies have pushed revenue to GDP so high as to be counterproductive for the economy. Nonetheless, the indicator is useful to watch, while keeping in mind the macroeconomic situation that may have the biggest impacts on revenue performance. It is generally awkward to come to the end of a TARP claiming that it implemented all of the components well, but that revenue remained stagnant or declined.

It is counterproductive and confusing to look at ratios of two things that are under the revenue agency's control and should be increasing, such as revenues paid on time or revenues assessed, as in Bulgaria's TARP. Overall success or failure might not change the ratio. Or differentials in the relative success or failure of the numerator and denominator could move the indictor in misleading ways.

## Borrower Context

Besides what is in the project itself, success depends on how the project is situated in the borrower country—government and society—and in the Bank's system. Designing and implementing a successful revenue reform requires understanding the micro political economy of taxpayers and the tax administration. A macro political science overview is usually not as important. This section takes up the borrower context, and the next discusses the Bank context.

### Reform Commitment

The commitment of both the minister of finance and the revenue agency are essential for project success. In Vietnam, the two could not agree on the project implementation plan, leading to its failure. In Mexico, the minister of finance supported the TARP strongly and made the revenue agency (SAT) independent from the Undersecretariat for Revenue, which had been a politicizing influence.

In Bulgaria, the Tax Department refused even to meet with the IMF–World Bank team that was diagnosing the situation. So, after the prime minister asked the Bank to do a lending project to implement the IMF recommendations, it was agreed to start an entirely new National Revenue Agency (NRA). The former Tax Department was shut down, and its employees were let go, although the qualified ones were eligible to reapply. The Tax Department had a much smaller staff and fewer decentralized offices, which were allegedly the locus of much corruption. The new NRA and the Ministry of Finance worked enthusiastically to implement the TARP, contributing fundamentally to its success.

While administrative reform aims to make filing and payment easier from the payers' point of view, a key objective of the projects supported by the Bank has been to raise more revenue—getting households and firms to pay as much tax as they legally owe, which is more than many of them had been paying. This always arouses some opposition. The reforms then can succeed only if the top political figures are willing to support measures to collect from the rich and powerful—often their friends and family. Dialogue to clarify this commitment needs to come at the beginning of the project; in the successful cases, the dialogue has focused on the need to finance social and infrastructure expenditures that will be politically popular and economically beneficial.

### Turnover of Counterparts

Since a typical TARP lasts five to seven years, it is necessary to prepare for some turnover of political leadership, perhaps even at the head of the revenue agency. To deal with this change, the project team should develop a broad consensus for the TARP, particularly in the ministry and the revenue agency. In Bulgaria, the project had strong support from the top technocrats in the NRA. When there was turnover at the top of the ministry and the NRA, the NRA technocrats worked with the Bank team to prepare briefings for the new officials, ensuring that the project moved forward despite changes at the top.

In Indonesia, the project initially had support at the very top, but when personnel there changed, the project languished and died because it did not have wider support in the government or society. The TARP in Mexico benefited from continuity, as the new head of the SAT came on board when implementation started and remained there through the project's duration and beyond.

### Governance and Anticorruption Strategy

Tax administration—collecting money from private firms and households—creates opportunities and incentives for corruption. Although corruption is common, the usual need to develop a tax administration project with tax administration personnel makes it difficult to face the problem of corruption directly. Indeed, preventing corruption from derailing the project can become challenging.

Indonesia's TARP faced a corruption nexus between the taxpayers and tax agents, which had created a conflict of interest about reforming the revenue administration. The problem was not understood during project preparation and never dealt with during seven years of attempted implementation. This contributed to the complete failure of the project to implement or disburse.

In Guatemala, corruption by one head of the tax agency temporarily derailed the project. This was eventually corrected by bringing in a new head and sending his predecessor to jail. The experience points to the need for the project to have governance and anticorruption goals and for the World Bank to continue its engagement in countries where governance is weak.

- Does a separate higher pay scale for personnel of the revenue authority help to reduce corruption? When, if ever, has having one been necessary or helpful for reforming revenue administration? In Mexico, public sector salaries were adjusted (in the 1990s), so no special salary scale was needed in the SAT.
- Should tax administration reform be integrated with broader governance reform? Would doing so be useful or a distraction and unneeded complication?

## World Bank Context

For a task team leader (TTL) or a TTL's manager, the World Bank Group has its own changeable political economy within which a TARP must be developed and implemented. Here we address four common issues: determining staffing, keeping expectations realistic, deciding which Bank unit will manage the project, and coordinating with other donors.

### Staffing

Around 1990, the Bank made a strategic decision to divide the work in public finances so that the Bank would focus on public spending and the IMF would focus on taxes, for which it already had a lot of expertise in the Fiscal Affairs Department. Subsequently, the (few) Bank staff who had been working on taxes moved on to other topics. Since 2000, the Bank has brought in a few tax and customs specialists, although not enough to keep pace with the growth in tax work that the Bank has undertaken, and the IFC has brought in some tax specialists for its advisory services work on business taxation.

### Realistic Expectations

One common error with a reform of revenue administration is to make optimistic projections about how much extra revenue it will generate and to use these to make optimistic, "high-case" projections for macrofiscal balances. Doing this has usually led to disappointment and disillusion, because even a well-designed and well-implemented revenue administration reform rarely brings quick results in the timeframe of a DPL. When revenue rises quickly, it is usually due to exogenous macroeconomic events, which should be discounted when assessing the effects of revenue administration reform.

Similarly, the expected length of the project needs to be realistic and not counted on to be completed quickly, because the reorganization and reorientation of personnel—the real core of any reform in the public sector—takes time.

Rushing it creates resistance and puts people into situations where they are not prepared to perform adequately. Even when the former agency is totally scrapped and a new one is created, doing so takes at least as much time as reforming an existing organization. Thus, to keep counterparts moving, the projected length of a project should at least be realistic given continuation of the conditions at project preparation. And management has to realize that extensions may be needed to deal with unanticipated complications.

### Allocation of Tax Work within the World Bank Group

Three Global Practices have inherited most of the Bank's work on tax policy and administration: Governance (from former PREM, public sector policy group), Macroeconomics and Fiscal Management (from former PREM, economic policy group), and Trade and Competitiveness (former IFC business taxation advisory services). As noted, these units have traditionally had different motives for working on tax administration.

The PREM public sector and economic policy groups were in the same department before the latest reorganization and usually worked closely together, often seamlessly under the direction of the same PREM sector leader in the country department. Although some of the tax administration work was solely analytic and diagnostic, often through participation in an IMF tax mission, PREM's work on tax administration typically aimed to prepare a lending project—a TARP, typically for amounts up to US$100 million. The successful series of tax activities in Kazakhstan consisted of analytical and advisory activities (AAA) co-financed (more than half) by the country. This business model is similar to and was merged to some extent with IFC's advisory services.

Given the rarity of true tax specialists in the Bank, the task manager of a TARP was usually a public sector specialist or a country economist. Country economists from the economic policy group typically emphasized the need to raise revenue to pay for public expenditure. Both units were very aware of this need because of their joint work on public expenditure reviews. For the public sector policy group, revenue administration fit in with other work on public financial management, civil service, and anticorruption. Now that the former public sector and economic policy personnel—public sector specialists and country economists—are separated into different Global Practices, coordinating their efforts will require more deliberate effort.

The IFC's business taxation advisory services is called nonlending technical assistance in the Bank context, and these tasks (and personnel) have moved to the Bank as part of the Trade and Competitiveness Global Practice.

The IFC's work on business taxation had three components: core tax, transfer pricing, and tax transparency. Core tax encompassed analytical work and advisory services that aimed to reduce the overall burden of the tax system on the private sector in order to foster enterprise creation and inclusive growth. Specific topics included simplification of income tax policy and administration, tax legal and appeals reform, risk-based audit systems, reduction in the cost of complying with tax policies and procedures, elimination of discretion and legal ambiguity, and removal of barriers to the formalization of small businesses. The program's specific private sector focus allowed the IFC to carve a niche in the broad field of taxation reform.

The business taxation operations were not loans, but were financed by trust funds and, for middle-income countries, usually some client co-funding. They varied considerably in size, ranging from a minimum of US$40,000 to a maximum of US$5.1 million, with an average of about US$1 million. Sixteen projects were fully dedicated business taxation operations. In the other cases, business taxation activities were part of multiproduct projects, accounting for between 10 and 50 percent of total budgets.

### Coordination with Other Donors

Coordination with the IMF in doing TARPs has usually gone smoothly and benefited the project. In Bulgaria, the Bank's project was identified when the future TTL was participating in an IMF mission on taxation. Then IMF specialists joined in all of the preparation missions and in the supervision missions for the first year of implementation. Since the IMF only does diagnostic work and does not offer funding for implementation of administrative reform, there is minimal competition and much opportunity for synergistic cooperation.

With other donors, the division of labor is less clear and potentially less complementary. Bilateral donors and regional development banks have less technical capacity in tax administration and are often interested only in funding the implementation of projects. If this is known and planned for in advance, then the donor contribution can be a valuable source of co-financing for a Bank-led TARP. However, if this funding arrives after the TARP loan has been developed and approved, it can be disruptive and send mixed signals to the borrower about the need to reform administration in a logically integrated way. In Vietnam, for instance, some original parts of the TARP dropped out because other donors came in to fund them on a grant basis. This should have been planned, and the donor-funded parts should have remained integrated in substance with the overall project.

## World Bank Group Business Model for Work on Taxes

### Country Program Package on Taxation

A country's taxation performance is most likely to improve when the tax program combines AAA and investment technical assistance lending, and perhaps DPLs, according to some experts interviewed. This agrees with the preliminary results of the statistical analysis of the tax projects since 2000, which are presented in appendix C. Although the investment loan and AAA would cover most of the details of improving administration and performance, having a DPL may succeed in getting sufficient attention and thus action on reforms—like closing loopholes in tax laws.

However, merely having a DPL with some prior actions on tax matters, but no complementary and longer-lasting support through an investment loan, usually has not produced good results. The Bank cannot force a country to do something against the government's will—as painful experience has shown—but the Bank can encourage a government to move more promptly on what it wants to do eventually. When a DPL task team lines up the prior actions, the Bank can say that, in order to count a tax reform action, there also needs to be a longer-term investment project to facilitate sustained implementation.

Getting the best results from assistance on taxes requires coordination among all of the World Bank Group units working on taxes in a country. In some cases in the past, this has happened, with beneficial effects for the country. Sometimes the country team has orchestrated this collaboration, but not always. Now, however, the move of the former IFC business taxation advisory services into the World Bank and the creation of the Tax Group (spanning the relevant Global Practices) could enable more systematic coordination. An instrument for coordination is thus coming into existence, and senior management will need to insist that it be used.

### Coordination with the IMF and Others

The IMF has a great store of expertise, on which the Bank has often drawn. It cannot always mobilize at short notice, however, so the Bank teams planning to work on taxes should make contact and plans with the IMF far enough in advance so that the IMF expertise can come in on time.

With other institutions that might provide support for tax reform, such as the regional development banks and some bilateral donors, the World Bank's country offices can stay alert for any news that the others are launching tax projects and then make sure that efforts are coordinated.

### Funding for Work on Taxation

Unlike 20 years ago when funding for almost all tax work by Bank staff and consultants came from the Bank budget, much of the funding now comes from the middle-income client government itself (on some fee-for-service or shared financing basis) or from external grants. These grants are more often for work in low-income countries, but some are for work in middle-income countries.

As these non-Bank budget funds increase in importance, which seems likely, the standards and processes for obtaining and allocating funds need to become more transparent and fair and less dependent on the connections and entrepreneurial spirit of the individual TTL.

### Notes

1. It remains to be seen the extent to which this attitude passes along to the Trade and Competitiveness Global Practice, which largely inherited the advisory services work on business taxation.
2. The incentive is particularly strong if the alternative tax is a flat annual fee, the burden of which diminishes to zero as firm size increases. This problem is especially prevalent in Europe and Central Asia.

3. In the third quarter of the twentieth century, national governments in Argentina, Brazil, Colombia, and Mexico centralized most state, provincial, and departmental taxes into the national VAT. In return, the intermediate (and to a lesser extent local) governments got formula-based transfers. Although larger Brazilian states and recently Argentine provinces have shown strong interest in raising revenue, the exchange of taxation authority for transfers has generally reduced or eliminated subnational interest or political responsibility for making taxation efforts. Those subnational governments focus mostly on getting more transfers out of the national government.

4. Jit Gill was the task team leader for these projects in Jamaica, and a decade later, after he died, an award for reformers was created in his name. The first award went to Carlton Davis, who was the main Jamaican government counterpart.

5. They both used a system from Fast Enterprises called GenTax, which is also used in Poland and most U.S. states.

6. Many parts of the agency had their own systems for IT, data storage, personnel, procurement, and budgeting. Moving them to a unified IT platform served as an entry point to press for harmonization and unification of the other systems, which was the signature achievement of the project. This coordination required a lot of attention and effort from the Bank and SAT teams and especially from a large team of consultants from the Mexican private sector, mostly Cemex, for which the SAT paid out of its own resources.

## Reference

Bird, Richard, and Milka Casanegra de Jantscher, eds. 1992. *Improving Tax Administration in Developing Countries*, 19th ed. Washington, DC: International Monetary Fund.

## Environmental Benefits Statement

The World Bank Group is committed to reducing its environmental footprint. In support of this commitment, we leverage electronic publishing options and print-on-demand technology, which is located in regional hubs worldwide. Together, these initiatives enable print runs to be lowered and shipping distances decreased, resulting in reduced paper consumption, chemical use, greenhouse gas emissions, and waste.

We follow the recommended standards for paper use set by the Green Press Initiative. The majority of our books are printed on Forest Stewardship Council (FSC)–certified paper, with nearly all containing 50–100 percent recycled content. The recycled fiber in our book paper is either unbleached or bleached using totally chlorine-free (TCF), processed chlorine–free (PCF), or enhanced elemental chlorine–free (EECF) processes.

More information about the Bank's environmental philosophy can be found at http://www.worldbank.org/corporateresponsibility.

green
press
INITIATIVE

www.ingramcontent.com/pod-product-compliance
Lightning Source LLC
Chambersburg PA
CBHW080425270326
41929CB00018B/3166